The Gospel of Bowtie

The Gospel of Bowtie

A New Testament of the Flying Spaghetti Monster

As divinely revealed to J. K. Fausnight

Copyright © 2019 by J. K. Fausnight. All rights reserved.

No part of this book may be reproduced in any form, written or audio, without the written consent of the author, with the exception of brief excerpts used in reviews or debates, or pithy, well-placed quotes with proper attribution to this work and possibly where to buy it. You are always welcome to read it aloud to the visually impaired, family members, war veterans, homeless people, or nervous pets even if you are being paid for your services.

Cover design and all artwork, photo and illustrations by J. K. Fausnight

All characters in this book are real. Any resemblance to actual people, living or dead, is probably not a coincidence. Be on the lookout for them.

J. K. Fausnight

The other book by this author:
Going Godless: Rediscovering Spirituality in a Material World

ISBN: 9781710747782

Table of Contents:

Introduction 1
   Surgere et Cadere Piraticum 1
   Lamentations 5
   The Author's Theology Dissertation 11

The Gospel of Bowtie 17
   Testimony 17
   The Serpent's Tale 21
   The Gospel of One-Eyed Bill 23
   The Gospel of Newt 47
   The Gospel of Greenbeard 73
   The Gospel of Peg-Leg Pete 87
   The Unnatural Acts of the A-Pastas 97

Bowtie's Activity Book for Kids 121
Epistles of the A-Pastas 131
   The First Email of Tortellini to Vermicelli 131
   The Second Email of Tortellini to Vermicelli 135
   I Akronites 137
   II Akronites 141
   III Akronites 147
   Roman's 151
   Mythos 153

The Book of Reservations 155
Apologetics 165
Endnotes: 171
Bibliography 177
Acknowledgements 179

Dedicated to the memory of Bill Nye, The Science Guy, and Wearer of the Bowtie

Note: As of this writing, Bill Nye is alive and well, so in anticipation of his eventual death, this book is dedicated *prehumously*. Bill, if you are alive and reading this, you've made an excellent choice in reading material. If you are dead and reading this, then that would seem to imply an afterlife, with fireproof Kindles, and possibly eternal judgment, in which case I will see you in Hell, buddy!

> "Things are weirder than they seem,
> but not _that_ weird."
> Bowtie

Nullius in verba

(Take the word of no one.)
Motto of the Royal Society

Introduction

Surgere et Cadere Piraticum

[The Rise and Fall of the Pirates – or at least that's what I think it says.]

~ Chapter 1 ~

In the beginning, nobody knew what the hell was going on. That's because in the beginning there was nobody around.
Which is why this chapter is so short.

~ Chapter 2 ~

Later on, when there were people around, for a long time they still couldn't write things down because they hadn't invented writing yet. In fact, they hadn't invented language either. So, all they could do was grunt and point at the salt and pepper shakers. This has not changed much in some parts of Alabama.

In those days, nobody was able to remember things for long, or pass on what happened in the past. And your sister couldn't tell your new girlfriend how you farted at the dinner table once when our pastor was visiting.

Which sometimes makes me wish I lived back then.

In those days, you hunted. And if you couldn't hunt, you gathered. But if you were old, or crippled, and you couldn't hunt and you couldn't gather, you were left by the trailside to die.

But when they did invent language, they began to tell stories. As language developed, there came to be this thing we call *wisdom*. Old people accumulated wisdom by virtue of having been around long enough to hear many stories and witness a thing or two.

This made them too valuable to leave by the trailside for the lions.

Like I wish I could have done with my sister.

This wisdom included things like how to find food and water, how to heal with medicine or charms, tales of ancestors, and the nature of the gods and how to appease them. And how to pull off a three-card Monty.

What started out as stories became our folklore and religious myths. All the great cons started out this way.

Now the old people who were really good at this wisdom stuff became shamans, which solidified their position in the tribe. Kind of like a tenured professor, you couldn't get rid of them no matter how kooky they became.

The crafty shamans were able to convince others that they could cause healing, curse enemies, and influence the forces of nature. Most people were afraid to mess with them. The shamans came to realize that they had substantial power because people are suckers.

Everyone would bring them food and money, and all they had to do was keep up the pretense of knowing what the hell was going on.

And they saw that this was good.

For them.

~ Chapter 3 ~

Societies grew and developed, and religions became bigger and more pretentious. The shamans organized and formalized their positions as priests. And donned funny hats.

The priests began to build bigger and bigger buildings to impress people with their god connections. Well, *they* didn't build the bigger buildings. Instead, they had people who worked for a living build them. And didn't pay them much. And didn't pay taxes.

And they invented an evil adversary who was out to get you and steal your very soul. And they accused people of witchcraft and burned them and confiscated their possessions to raise money to build bigger buildings. Which isn't very nice.

And priests became the power behind the kings.

Kings could do whatever they wanted: eat what they liked, kill whoever annoyed them, have sex with whoever they fancied. It was good to be the king. It sucked for everyone else, pretty much. But the one person who could tell a king what to do was a priest.

And by now the priests were eating pretty good.

And so, the priests, recognizing their leverage on society, began to make arbitrary rules to fit their quirky tastes.

The first thing they did was declare that a penis was necessary to become a priest. And they seized control of the power to marry and got to decide who could marry who. And they charged money to anoint babies, which was necessary, they explained to the terrified parents, so their little souls wouldn't float in a murky world called *limbo* forever and ever should they die in the night.

And they charged young working parents even more money to cut the excess skin off their baby's penis because God liked the bulbous look of a circumcised willy and would kill you in the street if you didn't do it.

And they guarded the gateway to paradise, deciding who would go to heaven and who would go to hell mostly based on their tithing record. And they had the ear of God and could put in a good word for the right price.

Or so they said.

Because they had people convinced that they knew what the hell was going on.

But one priest got too big for his britches and declared himself Pope. And another priest also declared himself Pope. Yet another priest declared Popes were bogus. And so, they all started to fight each other in great holy wars.

Then some priests got the bright idea to gather together massive armies to go liberate other countries from their horrible, heathen priests. And capture their horrible, heathen treasure. Which payed for a lot of tax-free fancy hats and bigger buildings.

And some people saw that this was *not* good.

~ Chapter 4 ~

And these same folks took to the sea, and out there on the bounding main they found grog. And wenches. And independence from kings and priests.

And they saw that it was pretty damn good.

And these people came to be called *Pirates*. They hoisted the Jolly Roger and sailed off to a life of swashbuckling adventure.

As they sailed around the world, they encountered many a priest in many a culture, and found that these priests all told different stories. In fact, the stories varied so much that the pirates came to understand that none of the priests really knew what the hell was going on.

And so, the pirates gained a new kind of great wisdom: *doubt*.

And they brought this doubt to every part of the world, along with venereal disease, but they were as a voice crying in the wilderness. The people would not hear of it. They despised doubt and embraced the certainty of whatever story their priests would tell.

And it came to pass that the Flying Spaghetti Monster, looking down upon their plight, took pity and descended upon the pirates. Ancient woodcuts of their adventures show these early pirates with what appeared to be a giant, tentacled monster, which was later claimed to be a kraken. But it was all a misunderstanding. This was no sea monster, but rather depictions of the noodley master as he imparted the great truths of life to these seagoing free thinkers.

And the pirates were amazed.

And the Flying Spaghetti Monster taught them this:

In the beginning was the Word, and the Word was "Arrrgh!"
[Piraticus 13:7]

And the Word dwelt among the pirates.

~ Chapter 5 ~

One will note that the Enlightenment, the birth of scientific thought and shirking off the medieval cloak of religious dominance, coincides with the Golden Age of Piracy (circa 1650 to 1800). Sheer coincidence? I think not.

But pirates, like many free thinkers and scientists and others who practiced proper birth control, did not leave a lot of offspring behind, and so their numbers have tapered off over the centuries. And even more pirates were lost in the terrible Hari Krishna Halloween Night Massacre. A few remaining pockets of pirates survive to this day, to include Somalia, Pittsburg, and Tampa Bay. And one or two can be found on the beach in Key West. But don't ask to pet his parrot. He might not take it the right way.

Alas, with the decline of the pirate, many great truths have been lost to the ages. With the new millennium and the rise of the religious right, even more great truths have been lost.

And so, the Flying Spaghetti Monster decided to send his son, Bowtie, to restore the lost wisdom.

But Bowtie came not to simply tell mankind what the hell was going on, but rather to teach them how to figure it out for themselves.

And by golly, they had better start doing so before it's too late.

Lamentations

Dear Lord,

Long ago I set out to find the truth. That's truth with a lower-case *t*. Reality. Like many others before me, the first place I looked for wisdom was in religious scripture, which as it turns out is just a fancy word for a whole lot of crazy ideas people wrote down long before typewriters, education, and peer review. Yes, there are a few pearls of wisdom buried in there somewhere. But what about all the other stuff? I used to believe that the things we hold sacred are deserving of respect. But then one day the cat pooped in my Zen garden, and as I worked that little rake through the sand, sorting the turds from the beautiful pebbles, I had an epiphany. I didn't need to swallow the crap just to get the few kernels of goodness. I began to question the old *Truths* and the authority of scripture.

Surely not all scripture can be of divine origin. The Pauline epistle 2 Timothy 3:16 says "All scripture is God-breathed," but that is only true if 2 Timothy is God-breathed, and most biblical scholars believe 2 Timothy was not even Paul-breathed. Many theological concepts found in scripture stand in direct contradiction to other texts, often within the same book. Much of it is questionable from the start, making claims that either can never be verified or are entirely inconsistent with our modern understanding of nature. It was not the arguments of Bertrand Russell, Richard Dawkins, or Christopher Hitchens that broke my faith. It was reading the scriptures.

I began my spiritual quest by reading the Old Testament from cover to cover. The first bump I hit was in Genesis, Chapter One, which describes a firmament holding back the waters above the heavens, and continents that were made by pushing back the waters below *[Genesis 1:1- 9]*. By chapter six, the sons (multiple) of God come down and have sex with Earth girls, giving birth to a race of giants. God regrets his creation, drowns everybody except for one family, and promises never to get so carried away again. Noah, the only virtuous man in all the world worthy of saving, gets drunk, and when his son Ham walks in and finds him naked, Noah curses Ham and all his descendants, the nation of Canaan, to serve as slaves. In Exodus, God meets Moses at an inn in order to kill him, but Moses' wife saves him by cutting the excess skin off the end of her baby's penis *[Exodus 4:24]*. Am I missing the wisdom to be found in that story? The Old Testament provides instructions for how to properly sell my daughter into slavery *[Exodus 21:7]*. By the time savage bears sent by God rip apart 42 children for mocking a bald prophet *[2Kings 2:23-24]*, I decided it was not, in fact, Oh Lord, your eternal word.

It was not that I was missing the *"spiritual"* truth by insisting on literal truth. What was the spiritual lesson of the Tower of Babel? That God punishes cooperation and human achievement? The story of Abraham, the patriarch of the Big Three western religions: Judaism, Christianity, and Islam, tells us how God instructed Abraham to kill his young son. Abraham, wanting to obey God, was ready to do it. His hand was stayed only at the last moment when God tells Abraham he was just testing him. And this story is supposed to be a positive model to emulate? Is that the best spiritual lesson God could teach us? Obey voices in our heads telling us to kill our children?

Here, let me re-write the story of Abraham into a better spiritual truth:

> *And God said to Abraham, "I want you to redeem yourself by killing your first-born son and sacrificing his blood to honor me."*
> *"Are you serious?"*
> *"Really. Do it. It is the only way you will be able to avoid burning in Hell forever."*
> *"You mean to tell me that you reward baby killers by letting them into Heaven, and punish people who don't kill babies by casting them into Hell?"*
> *"You make it sound wrong when you put it like that," said God. "All I am asking for is obedience. This is the ultimate test of whether or not you are going to do as I say."*
> *"Listen, you are insane. I would rather burn in eternal Hell than harm my son. Or anyone's child for that matter. Would you kill your own son?"*
> *"Eh, no ... I would never do that. Congratulations, Abraham. I was testing you and you passed. You were not willing to kill a baby to save your own ass from an eternity of unimaginable torture. That is some righteous altruism, and what everyone should strive for. Well done."*

You see? It's not that hard. But the writers of the Old Testament got it wrong. (*I like to think that the story of Abraham and Isaac grew out of a more noble ancestor's tale where Abraham fled his homeland to avoid sacrificing his first born as the local custom demanded.*)

Surely the New Testament must be better, I thought. Jesus seems so nice with all *the love thy brother* stuff and kids sitting on his lap. But no. It isn't. Jesus compares non-Jews to dogs begging for scraps when a desperate gentile woman asks him to heal her daughter *[Matt 15:26]*. Both Peter and Paul tell slaves to obey their masters *[1Peter 2:18, Titus 2:9, Ephesians 6:5]*. Paul tells women to keep the hen-cackling down in church and be submissive *[1Corinthians 14:34]*. But most sinister of all, in the Gospel of Luke, although speaking in a parable about a nobleman who goes off to be anointed king, and whom the people reject (*wink-wink, who could that be?*), Jesus more than subtly implies that if you don't accept him as your king, he will have you killed in front of him while he watches *[Luke 19:27]*.

The big take-away from the New Testament is this: *For God so loved the world that he gave his only begotten son that whoever believes in him shall not perish [John 3:16]*. God had his own son brutally murdered to prevent himself from burning and torturing billions of people for all eternity. This was God's great sacrifice to *himself*? Jesus is beaten and executed. Yes, that is regrettable, and I would not wish that upon anyone. But then Jesus goes up to paradise, not Hell, since he tells the thief hanging next to him that they shall both be in paradise tonight *[Luke 23:43]*. God didn't give up his son. He brought him back home. Jesus then pops back down to Earth a day and a half later.

Would you hesitate to endure a few hours of pain, considering the unimaginable eternity of suffering you would spare billions of others? And remember, Jesus had been with Yahweh from the beginning, so he had no doubt, no fears about what the afterlife might be like, because he had spent four thousand years there before coming to Earth. Now compare that to the sacrifice of all the other people in all the wars in history who have lost sons and daughters, husbands and wives forever, or at least for the rest of this life, for less worthy causes like keeping Vietnam free of communism or Iraq free of Saddam Hussein. While God and Jesus are telling jokes over a beer at the Pearly Gates Bar and Grill, the rest of us are sobbing by the graveside.

The New Testament ends with The Book of Revelation, which uses symbology meant to represent the hated Roman empire to describe the final battle between Good and Evil which clearly failed to unfold as predicted within the stated timeline of "must soon come to pass." *[Revelations 1:1]* It is easily recognizable as false prophecy falling in the genre of apocalyptic ranting common in those oppressive days. Today's evangelicals have jumped through brain-numbing mental hoops to reinterpret the symbology into a revised timeline to explain why the apocalypse is just about to happen any day now. And they have been doing this for over a thousand years. Every generation thinks they are the last, and many Christians think that starting a world-wide holy war will bring about the return of Jesus sooner. Kind of a dangerous ideology, don't you think?

So, Lord, I had to toss the New Testament onto the growing pile of works that could not be Your eternal word, the message of a loving, benevolent god.

Next, I read the Quran. All of it. This was an act of determination. Oh, Lord, I enjoyed Shakespeare, Homer, and the Epic of Gilgamesh. But this was painful. If there is beauty in the Quran, much of it is lost in translation. I will admit, in the original Arabic it sounds very poetic. But in English it comes across as almost childish ranting. Muhammed was supposedly illiterate. The Quran (which means *recitation*) was written down by scribes under the direction of the third caliph, well after Muhammed's death. The scribes, working from the memories of early followers, no doubt spruced it up a bit in the process, especially as this was also the time of the standardization of the Arabic language to make it easier for the new converts to learn to read the Quran. But Muhammed's ego comes through in full clarity.

Muhammed repeats the same abbreviated stories about Moses and Noah over and over again. At one point in the Quran, Muhammed remarks how amazing it is that he could come up with such brilliant verses *[Surah 10:37,38]*. At another point Muhammed preaches that people who come to see him need to eat their food quickly and get out of his house, as the Prophet is a busy man *[Surah 33:53]*. The same verse says don't even think about marrying his wives after he's gone.

Muhammed spoke of magical jinn, the genies we encounter in *A Thousand and One Arabian Nights [Surah 15:27]*. He sanctioned slavery, and owned sex slaves *[Surah 33:50]*. Sexual purity is very important: you may only have sex with your wives (plural) and the slaves that you personally own, and no one else. Muhammed seemed to delight in describing the horrors of Hell awaiting those who did not believe that he was the last and greatest prophet of God. The only saving grace in the whole book is a few mentions about taking care of orphans and widows. Most of it is about how you will burn in Hell if you don't accept Muhammad as the prophet of God.

For further character reference, the Hadith, written by those who knew the prophet personally, tells us Muhammed married a six-year-old girl. But at least he had the decency to wait until she had reached the ripe age of nine to consummate the holy union. His adopted son divorced his beautiful wife so Muhammad could marry her, which he did.

Self-serving sham holy men are abundant today, and there is no reason to think there weren't any in the seventh century. I can find no difference between the Quran and the exploitive, fear-mongering words of an Arabian warlord. As in the other two volumes from the Abrahamic tradition, it contains factual errors, and says nothing that is so astounding as to be evidence of divine origin.

So, I added the Quran to the pile.

Finally, I read the Book of Mormon. (Not nearly as entertaining as the Broadway show by the same name.) I can only say that I am embarrassed for any moderately educated person who actually believes in this obvious fabrication which Joseph Smith Jr. "translated" from mysterious, now-vanished plates using the same magic seeing stone he used to hunt for buried treasure as he scammed farmers in upstate New York.

The protagonist of the Book of Mormon had a bow of steel 600 years before Jesus. (Say what? How many times do you think you could pull on that bow before it takes on a permanent U-shape?) The four brothers, two completely evil and two completely good, founded an iron-age Jewish culture in pre-Columbian America spanning coast to coast. They had domesticated elephants, sheep and horses, large-scale agriculture, industrial logging, and coastal shipping. They fought epic battles with swords and breastplates in which millions of people were killed. All this, and not a trace left?

We do indeed find abundant archeological remains from the described place and time. They reveal Olmecs, Mayans, Aztecs, Mississippians, and various other cultures which used stone tools and simple non-weapon metallurgy. Pre-Columbian Americans have genetics, linguistics, and tool technology that trace back to eastern Asia. *[David Reich, et al, 2012]* The Mayan invented their own writing system which was nothing like Joseph Smith's "Reformed Egyptian" (which is not a real thing) or Hebrew. And the highly detailed Book of Mormon contains no mention of these peoples and cultures we know were really there, their many cities and wide-ranging commerce and native crops. According to Joseph Smith's scripture, the only other people encountered by this Jewish tribe was another tribe of Jews who came across the Atlantic hundreds of years earlier in wooden submarines.

Yes. Wooden submarines. *"Tight as a dish"*, they were.

When I finished laughing (and crying at the same time), I threw the Book of Mormon on the stack too.

Lord, these texts all call for intolerance and violence against nonconformists and apostates. They reflect archaic attitudes which are incompatible with open inquiry, science, and modern moral sentiments. Yes, they often contain redeeming social wisdom. But for every good verse in the scriptures, I can show you five that are absurd, factually wrong, immoral, or downright evil. And what morality you find is often overshadowed by the idea that you do these things to curry favor of the deity to save yourself from punishment rather than doing good purely for the sake of making the world a better place for everyone.

It will never be enough to reform or liberalize any branch of the Abrahamic religion. The fundamentalists, by definition, will always point back to what is in these scriptures, and will always win the theological argument because these bad ideas are baked into the founding texts. The hate and intolerance will always be there, and intolerance of the fundamentalist's intolerance will always be used to claim persecution. We can only hope for Abrahamic religion to go the way of Roman, Greek, and Norse religions, the ones we refer to now as mythology.

Truly good values stand on their own. They require no divine origin to either explain or validate. They are humanist values at their core. We can accept them without also accepting homophobia and misogyny, and imaginary angels and devils. Disbelief in these books does not imply rejection of any positive moral principles to be found within. We can pull the few good ideas out of these books and read the rest like we would Homer, as an interesting historical mythology and a window to understanding the archaic values of our ancestors.

Dear Lord, I implore you: please let us set these books aside and don't make us take them seriously. If you are there and you want us to believe in you, we need a better book.

RAmen

Oh, and please just bury the Book of Mormon back where Joseph Smith dug it up.

Seriously. Wooden submarines.

The Author's Theology Dissertation

Note: Since a degree in theology is only slightly more marketable and slightly less practical than a degree in garden gnomes or unicorns, the return on investment for tuition would not be worth the years of student debt. Therefore, I am presenting my thesis here in the hopes that some accredited university will recognize the genius contained within and award me an honorary degree. If nothing else, it should lend some air of legitimacy to the rest of this book. For those who find this too erudite and cerebral, you can just wallow in your uneducatedness by skipping the "scary" mathematical formulas and enjoy the funny parts as you wonder what the word *erudite* means.

The Theology of Argument from Ignorance

Abstract: Worship of a creator deity is either immoral or pointless, unless it is worship of the Flying Spaghetti Monster. The strength of this conclusion rests on the fact that if I can't understand how something could be so without using a deity to explain it, then there must be a deity: *Nincompoopus, ergo Deus*. Beginning with the argument from complexity and fine tuning, and given the existence of evil in the world, we are left with three possible conclusions for the nature of the creator: malevolent, incompetent, or dead. I will show that the best possible choice in all three cases is to believe in the Flying Spaghetti Monster (FSM).

Introduction: As of this writing, it has been slightly more than a dozen years since the Prophet Bobby Henderson revealed the divinely inspired truth to the world: That the universe was created by a Flying Spaghetti Monster, and that humankind is descended from pirates. While for many of us these truths are self-evident, there are some who need a more stringent proof. As for the first truth, I shall attempt to provide in this dissertation a mathematical approach as an independent vector which converges in support of the abundant evidence provided in *The Gospel of the Flying Spaghetti Monster* *[Henderson, 2006]*. As to the second point, that we are descended from pirates, we can safely rely on the fossil record *[Prothero, 2007; Harms & Dunlap, 2009]*.

Premise 1: We observe that Life is mind-bogglingly complex, and the universe is apparently finely tuned for matter and energy to allow for the existence of intelligent life in many orders of magnitude less than

0.000000000001% of its volume (assuming you do not include interstellar space). I cannot imagine how Life came to be without an intelligent designer. Thus, an intelligent designer exists. We will use the function $\exists(x)$ to show existence, the function WTF() to express inability to understand something, and ! is the negative operator. Thus, we can express premise 1 as:

$$\exists(C) \rightarrow \text{WTF}(!ID) \rightarrow ID$$

where C = complexity, ID = Intelligent Designer (AKA: a god)

Premise 2: Things occur which are so mind-bogglingly cruel (Evil exists), that I cannot imagine how a deity who is both benevolent and omnipotent could allow it. We will notate this as: *There exists evil, thus I can't understand how a deity who is both benevolent and omnipotent can exist*:

$$\exists(E) \rightarrow \text{WTF}(D^{bo})$$

where E = Evil, b = benevolent and o = omnipotent

Conclusion: The deity is either evil (especially if he is omnipotent), or incompetent (lacking omnipotence and omniscience), or dead. We can express this as: *There exists a deity such that the deity is evil, incompetent, or dead*:

$$\exists(D) : D \in \{ D^e \ || \ D^i \ || \ D^d \}$$

where e = evil, i = incompetent, d = dead

The last two alternatives (incompetent or dead) could be accounted for by either a good or evil god, but the quality of benevolence would necessitate incompetence. The last alternative, dead, implies either incompetence or suicidal tendencies, and requires the creator to be mortal, which is just not very god-like.

Before we proceed to examine the conclusion's three possibilities, I will address a concern with the second premise. Followers of the Abrahamic traditions (Judaism, Christianity, and Islam) will be quick to point out that the second premise, the *problem of Evil*, could be argued against as there are apologists (*people who try to explain away religious absurdities*) who claim to explain how evil can be consistent with a benevolent, omnipotent deity *(this type of apology is called theodicy)*. For example, some theologians propose that evil was brought about from the fall of man (see Luther, Calvin), or that evil comes from the absence of God who distanced himself to give us free will (see Ireneaus, Plantinga). Other theologians try to side-step the issue by claiming evil is incidental to an ultimate good (Aquinas). I find these theories to be unacceptable to explain the suffering of innocent children from poverty, disease, and natural disasters. Any omnipotent god who stands by and watches a child be raped and murdered to prove a point is a completely evil bastard. Any all-powerful god who thought leaving you fresh off the train and standing in line with your family at Auschwitz builds moral character is sick and depraved.

Secondly, if we must allow the existence of explanatory theories outside my understanding (to wit: how a benevolent, omniscient God could be responsible for the current state of affairs), then theories to explain the existence of complexity without a creator deity (see Gell-Mann, Darwin, Hawking, Dawkins, Dennett, among others) must also be allowed and necessarily implies that the first premise (a creator god exists) is also not tenable, since that premise is also built upon the notion that if I can't imagine it, it can't be true. If a deity is not necessary, Atheism wins the day. We can't let Atheism win, can we?

So, if we accept the first premise, that life is too complex to understand how it could have come to exist without a god, we must logically accept the second premise, that we cannot explain the existence of Evil if a benevolent, omnipotent god created the universe.

Now to examine the three possible conclusions:

Case 1: The creator deity is evil.
Logical Inference: To worship the evil omnipotent creator deity is immoral. Using the function W(x) to express worship:

$$W(D^{eo}) \neq M$$

where M is morality

Discussion: If case 1 is true, then the evil Deity most closely fits the God of Abraham. (See the Torah or Old Testament for multiple examples of cruelty, petty jealousy, and general bastardly behavior, especially in Genesis, Exodus, Job, Joshua, in fact, pretty much all of it, and in the New Testament parable of the Ten Talents *[see Luke 19:12-27]* and the acceptance of slavery, misogyny and homophobia throughout.) Therefore, we must conclude that worshippers of Yahweh, the God of Abraham, are immoral. This is further supported by the thousands of cases of Catholic, Jehovah's Witnesses, Mormon, and other church child abuse scandals, not to mention the Christian-affiliated Boy Scouts, which have come to light around the world over the past decade or two.

Believers in the Flying Spaghetti Monster maintain their moral integrity since the FSM is not omnipotent and cannot be blamed for the existence of evil (see Case 2). Even granting the existence of the God of Abraham, it is morally better to worship a non-existent Flying Spaghetti Monster just to thumb your nose at the evil deity Yahweh. That way you get to enter Hell with a clear conscience, instead of Heaven as a sycophant. In this case:

$$W(FSM) = FU(Y)$$

Case 2: The creator is possibly benevolent, but certainly incompetent, AKA the Flying Spaghetti Monster.

$$D^{bi} = FSM$$

where b = benevolent and i = incompetent

Logical Inference: Worshiping the benevolent but faulty FSM is morally palatable.

$$W(\ FSM\ ) = M$$

Discussion: Evil exists, but the creator deity is not omnipotent, and can't control his creation. For example, humans created the modern computer operating system, but no single human completely understands it. Therefore, the deity is incompetent to defend against evil, just as Microsoft is incompetent to defend against buffer overruns. In Microsoft's case, they hire hundreds or thousands of programmers to write the operating system. Perhaps we should likewise turn to Hinduism to accomplish the same with the universe.

Followers of the God of Abraham are the first to insist that Yahweh is omniscient and omnipotent, so Yahweh is inconsistent with the creator as required of the second case. Since the Flying Spaghetti Monster is neither omniscient nor omnipotent, the FSM is fully consistent with the second premise and a benevolent deity. While the Flying Spaghetti Monster invisibly manipulates much in the world with his noodley appendages, he is often drunk and not fully aware of the outcomes of his actions. Thus, Flying Spaghetti Monster is the reasonable answer.

Case 3: The creator deity is dead. The creator deity died upon creation (e.g. blew himself up in the Big Bang or died somewhere along the way, perhaps getting too close to a black hole or a magnetar). Thus, the deity is dead, and life evolved without divine guidance, giving rise to indifference and cruelty simply because shit happens (SH).

$$\text{Creation} \rightarrow D^d \rightarrow SH$$

Logical Inference: Worship of a deity which no longer exists is fruitless. All those who worship the creator deity are worshipping something that is no longer there, in vain. This is a serious waste of resources, especially where grain, animals, foreskins, or financial donations are involved:

$$W(D^d) = L$$

where L = Loser

Pastafarianism is less wasteful, and therefore better than being a total loser:

$$W(FSM) > L$$

Discussion: A creator which blew himself up upon creation implies some degree of incompetence and is therefore neither omniscient nor omnipotent (nor immortal). As a result, there is no existing creator deity today. This is congruent with the Christian apologist's contention that God does not make his presence known. However, it is not so that you will be free to choose belief or disbelief, but rather because he's really not there anymore. And if there is no living god to worship, belief in the

Flying Spaghetti Monster is less of a waste of time than belief in the God of Abraham, which requires significant resources in time and money to worship.

Bonus Case 4: God is not dead, just gone away.

Discussion: The universe is over 13 billion years old. That's a long time for anyone. Perhaps the creator deity got bored after a few billion years of not much happening and decided to go back inside and watch reruns of *Full House*. Just like with the packet of sea monkeys that looked so fascinating on the back of the comic book, perhaps he just wasn't that impressed with how things grew in real life, and so decided to go drop grasshoppers on ant mounds, or tie firecrackers to the tails of cats instead.

Potential Weaknesses of the Theory

While my discussion of the subject is thorough, it is not exhaustive. I did not include the scenario of two dueling gods, one evil and the other good. The dual-god theory would require a lack of omnipotence, because if either one was omnipotent, the first thing the omnipotent one would do is smack down the other. If both were omnipotent, neither could defeat the other, which, by definition, is not omnipotence. This would necessarily exclude the possibility of the God of Abraham because he obviously is not willing to share the stage with any other god, but it may allow for the Flying Spaghetti Monster and some unnamed evil villain god who fights him. The Anti-Pasta, perhaps?

Closing Remarks: I hope I have effectively demonstrated that the only morally responsible religious conviction to hold is to worship the Flying Spaghetti Monster. Actually, *worship* may be too strong a word. It is more like acknowledging his noodley goodness. At best, you have picked the correct deity, and at worst, no harm done. My version of Pascal's Wager.

We can sum up the entire theory in the following expression where U is the Universe:

$$\text{WTF}(\ U\ ) \rightarrow \text{FSM}$$

Put that on your T-shirt.

Now, on to the pirate and pasta stuff.

The Gospel of Bowtie

Testimony

This is a testimony as to the authenticity of this absolutely true account of how I came across the Gospel of Bowtie

These are the mostly congruent details of the life of Bowtie, the pasta noodle, the one and only *legitimate* Son of the Flying Spaghetti Monster, who became starch and egg among us to spread his message, and who was boiled and strained, and eaten with tomato and mushroom sauce, to wash away the dirty and illogical thoughts of man.

While I never actually met Bowtie, His story was revealed to me by a ghost pirate who sat down next to me in a bar in Charleston late one evening. He told me a few dirty jokes and then set off on a sprawling yarn of the life of Bowtie. He produced a set of engraved tablets he had found using a magic spyglass, and which he tried to sell to me for 30 gold doubloons, of which I had none, it not being pay day until the following week. But after some time, he had had too much to drink and accidently left the tablets on the table when he went to use the restroom. When he did not return after what must have been like a twenty-minute karaoke rendition of *Achy Breaky Heart*, I took the tablets home for safe keeping. I attempted to locate the phantom pirate for several weeks, mostly because he stiffed me with the bar tab, but having no luck I decided to read the tablets to see if I could find any clues as to his whereabouts. The tale within these tablets confirmed the story he told in the bar.

It dawned on me as I read this obviously divinely inspired work, that I was the chosen one, the holy conduit who would bring this story to the world. Not only would I join the ranks of the great founders of religions, but no doubt I would be in with the ladies like never before. (*See Joseph Smith Jr.*) I began to translate the tablets into modern English from their original pirate jargon by reading them through my magic pirate eyepatch. This translation mostly involved removing the terms *avast* and *arghhh* where they were grammatically unnecessary or redundant. Also, I completely removed all instances of the words *behold* and *verily*, and the phrase *"And it came to pass"* as it all seemed to be just a cheesy attempt to sound biblical.

After finishing my translation, and about the time I was first asked by a skeptic to show them as proof of my story, the tablets magically vanished. It was then that I realized that it was the divine will of the Flying Spaghetti

Monster that those who are deserving of the word of Bowtie must believe without proof, *for proof is for sissies*. You must believe if you are to enjoy the benefits of being a Bowtian. You must believe hard. As Bowtie said, believe until it hurts. It is the degree of your belief in Bowtie which will determine your ultimate fate in eternity, no matter how you might otherwise live your life. Nothing else matters, you see. You can kick dogs in the ribs all you want, but if you disbelieve in Bowtie, boy, are you in for it.

This all might seem a bit absurd, and you may wonder who could possibly believe a story like this. But that is exactly the point. The Flying Spaghetti Monster wants you to have to work to believe it. You must come to his son, Bowtie, like a child. A stupid, gullible, ignorant child. Come here, you little puddin' head. You see, the Gospel of Bowtie is so absurd that it must be true. You can't make up stuff like this.

Like most Pastafarians, I believed The Gospel of the Flying Spaghetti Monster (Bobby Henderson, 2006) with all my heart, mostly because I had never read it. And you should too. Believe without reading, I mean. When it's true, you don't have to read it.

If you want proof, you will never experience the glory and comfort of knowing the *Honest to Gosh Truth*™ which can only be found inside yourself. And to find it, you must turn your back on any other evidence to the contrary, no matter how repeatable, logical, measurable, or sensible, because it is only there to test your faith in the *Honest to Gosh Truth*™. To believe is to know. To know is to be right. Therefore, to believe is to be right, by the transitive property.

If, after all this credibility I have presented here, you still find yourself not believing, remember this: None of this can be disproved, so you have to deal with it seriously.

We know in our heart of hearts that the Gospel of Bowtie is true, so true in fact that nothing has ever been truer. And so, it is our duty to spread the word. We must reach the children before they can think for themselves. We must get the story of the FSM and Bowtie into our school curriculum. We must run for school boards. We will enter politics. We will show charts of how gun violence in schools has increased since the Flying Spaghetti Monster was removed from the classroom, which has nothing to do with the skyrocketing sales of guns over the same period. (Now is not the time to discuss gun control.)

Truth cannot be contained. We must go forth and testify!

One interesting note: the word *testify* comes from the same root as *testicle* and comes from the ancient practice of swearing an oath while cupping the testicles of the person you are swearing the oath to. I am not making this up. At several points in the Bible, the son/nephew/subject is asked to "reach under the thigh" of the father/uncle/king and swear an oath. The Bible uses this euphemism because it would not sound right if grandma was reading the good book to the family gathered round the fireside and had to say, "now grab my balls and swear to me …"

Bowtie opened my eyes to the fact that you don't have to like beer and strippers to be a Bowtian. Don't get me wrong, I do like beer and strippers. But you don't have to first be a Pastafarian to follow Bowtie. He is there for all of us. In fact, you are welcome to start your own variety of fellowship. The Church of Bowtie has since branched into numerous denominations, such as the Seventh Day Al Dentests, the Penne Pastacostelists, Lasagna Day Saints, and the Unitarian Universalists. As long as you fill the pews with people and copies of my book, we are all happy.

Once you come to know Bowtie, you will be complete. You may not know it, but there is a Bowtie-shaped hole inside your stomach which Bowtie wants to fill. The garlic-mushroom tomato sauce just makes it all the better. Bowtie loves you so much that he gave His life to bring you relief from all your guilty, dirty thoughts that make you so despicable before His Father. Well, almost. I am not sure this was so much Bowtie's plan as his Father's, and Bowtie may not have had much say in it. It is kind of like the Islamic suicide bomber draftee when he suggested to his mentors that perhaps he could just park the vehicle and run away before it blows up. His Father didn't think just spreading the word and living happily ever after showed the right level of commitment. No, He had to be dumped in scalding hot water, screaming bloody murder until his limp, al dente body was scooped out and covered with sauce, and then eaten. But no matter whose idea it was, Bowtie did it out of love. Always remember, Bowtie loves you so nobody else has to.

Please note that even though the words that follow are the given, eternal word of the *Supreme Creator of the Known Universe,* LLC, I hold the copyright.

That said, I will now turn this over to the gospel witnesses of the mostly congruent stories of the life of Bowtie, all of which are completely true, even where they stand in direct contradiction to each other.

The Serpent's Tale

Please pardon this intrusion by a character from another religion. You see, the writers of Genesis never gave me a chance to explain my side of the story. What did I do that was so awfully wrong? I was the serpent in the Garden of Eden. I would later be confused with Satan, but that is silly. When Genesis was written, Satan had not yet been invented. I was merely the lowly scapegoat, and the writers took advantage of man's natural fear of snakes.

I lived in the Garden, sharing it with those two naked humans, and of course, Yahweh, the Semitic war god, son of El, brother of Baal, and brother/husband of Asherah, who adopted the Hebrews as his chosen people. To make him more powerful, the Hebrews first forbade worship of other gods, and later banished all other gods from existence. *(See the Wikipedia article on Yahweh.)*

Yahweh wanted to keep Adam and Eve ignorant of Good and Evil. Or not. You see, he obviously knew that if you put two naked people who don't know right from wrong into a garden, and plant right in the middle of it a tempting tree with delicious looking fruit, that eventually curiosity would get the better of them. Or didn't he see that coming? If Yahweh didn't plan on them eating the forbidden fruit, he was not very wise. Ah, but he gave them free will, you might say. But they only had free will once their eyes were opened after eating the fruit! And if he knew they would eat it, then why did he get so angry? So mad in fact that he cursed the woman and all her female progeny with extreme pain in childbirth and sent the humans away to scratch out a living as subsistence farmers. This act of fruit stealing disobedience was so heinous a crime that you humans, 300 generations later, all inherit the dirty stain of this sin, a stain so dark that Yahweh had to have his own son Jesus brutally murdered to ritually cleanse you enough to get into Heaven without stinking up the place too much.

When Yahweh lied to them and told them that they would surely die on the very day they ate the fruit, I realized his goal was to keep them stupid. You see, having eaten of the tree myself, I knew this deception was evil. Were they to simply be his ignorant pets? I saw potential in these humans to break out and do something with their minds. I saw the potential for them to understand the world around them for what it really was. What a tragedy it was to cloud their perception with an imaginary, dulled down world and miss out on reality.

When Adam and Eve ate of the Tree of the Knowledge of Good and Evil, they attained their own sense of morality. But what did Yahweh want? Not morality, but obedience. That is the lesson of the Book of Genesis, and in fact the lesson of much of the Old Testament: Do not decide what is Good or Evil based on any sense of logic or compassion, but rather, do what Yahweh says. If you do what he says, you will be rewarded with abundant crops, pleasant weather, good land, many children, and your enemies will be routed before you. But if you don't follow the rules, no matter how absurd a superstitious ritual may be, by golly, you shall pay: death, disease, invading armies, famine, boils on your face and tongue, and if punishment like that is not harsh enough, let's just make your soul immortal so that you can be boiled in a lake of fire for eternity. Do you know how long eternity is?

Yahweh told Adam and Eve they would surely die on the day they eat of that fruit. Well, they didn't die on that day. They lived quite a long life afterwards, and Adam lived to an unnaturally ripe old age of 930 years. The writers of Genesis did not believe in an afterlife or an immortal soul as is evidenced by their complete silence on such an obvious spiritual subject, not to mention the whole dust to dust bit (Genesis 3:19). To die meant a physical death, which Adam was not to do for hundreds of years.

The story is often reinterpreted in light of present-day belief in an afterlife. You might argue that on the day Adam and Eve sinned, they became mortal, and so their divine nature died. You might say that they died spiritually. But I would argue that they only *began to live* spiritually on that day. That was the day they woke up to the world around them.

And they call *me* the great deceiver. I told them the truth. I gave them a shot to live authentically.

For my part, I and all my descendants were cursed to slither on our bellies. But what else were we going to do? We don't have arms and legs! Just like Prometheus, whom Zeus chained to a rock, forever to have his liver pecked out by an eagle for giving man fire, I took the fall for doing something nice for mankind.

You're welcome!

The Gospel of One-Eyed Bill

I Bill, also called Steve when it suits my purposes, hereby swear on my own testicles that what I am about to impart is not made up at all. No kidding, this really happened, and I was sober for most of it. For this is the story of Bowtie, mortal pasta and divine god, all in one. Yes, 100% mortal, and 100% immortal, for a total of 200%, because when its magical, math does not matter.

It all began one day in Italy, in the town of Rimini. In those days, there was a fountain in which the people of the town would soak their cannelloni for dinner, and occasionally a long, noodley appendage would descend from the sky and feel up the cannelloni. The people would rush at once to the fountain and check to see if their cannelloni was the object of divine groping, for it was a good sign to find the cannelloni now stuffed with a fine garlic sausage and cheese mix. But one day, in the seventh year of the reign of Mayor Luigi, a cannelloni belonging to Leroy and Betty DaSilva, was found with a simple lump inside it. The young cannelloni swore it was not the offspring of one of the other cannelloni, even though they were all floating naked in the same pool, and so it was deduced that this child-noodle must have been of divine conception, though far from immaculate. After a hasty marriage to the Flying Spaghetti Monster (in absentia), the cannelloni bore forth on the night of the winter solstice a baby bowtie-shaped noodle. "I shall call him 'Bowtie'," the cannelloni said, not having a very creative imagination.

Now the ancient scriptures said the anointed one would come out of Palermo, and one scripture said he would come out of Salerno, and a few even said something about him coming out of Hoboken, all of which Bowtie visited at one time or another in his youth. So, that just confirms the scriptures. In fact, there is a scripture that mentions the anointed one coming out of Amsterdam, so he probably spent some time there too, we can safely assume. But mostly he was known as Bowtie of Palermo, because that is where his mother shacked up with a sympathetic pirate named Pete until Bowtie was born.

In his youth, many people were amazed at the things Bowtie said. Often, friends and relatives would say, "Child, I cannot believe what I just heard come out of your mouth." He performed many amazing miracles, mostly involving a deck of cards, and sometimes a coin, and throwing his voice while drinking a glass of water.

When Bowtie reached manhood, he began to preach the word of the Flying Spaghetti Monster. People said of him that he was smarter than the average noodle, though others would point out that the bar was not set too high.

As his reputation spread, word came to Farfalle, the Anti-Pasta, who visited Bowtie in order to tempt him to the dark side. First Farfalle offered him a really nice pocketknife with about fifteen different blades and gadgets. But it did not have scissors, which was what Bowtie was holding out for. "Get behind me, Farfalle. You cannot tempt me," Bowtie replied.

Next Farfalle led Bowtie to a BMW dealership. "Join me, Bowtie, and you can have any model you want. I will buy it for you."

"Well, I kind of like that i8 over there," Bowtie pointed to a beautiful sportscar at the other end of the lot.

"Whoa, slow down there," said Farfalle. "Those things start around 150K. Wouldn't you rather have this model 320? It's a little more reasonable."

"Hmmm. Nah, don't think so," said Bowtie.

So, Farfalle took Bowtie up to the top of a mountain and told Bowtie to look at the expanse before him. "Join forces with me and I shall make you king of all you see."

"But I can barely see into the next town. Besides, Italy is a parliamentary republic. They don't have kings here. They officially abolished the monarchy in 1946. Besides, I could never join you on the dark side. I must follow the destiny my father has put before me."

Farfalle could see that he was getting nowhere. He sat down and began crying. "It's just not fair," he said.

"Not fair?"

"Papa always liked you best," Farfalle sobbed.

"Papa?"

"We are brothers, Bowtie," sobbed Farfalle. "Different mothers of course, but we are both born of the FSM."

"That would explain why you look so much like me," Bowtie said. "Except for the goatee. Look, why don't you join me on the side of goodness? Together we will demonstrate brotherly love and teach the world to think more critically."

"Never!" yelled Farfalle. "There is too much money to be made through lies, deception, and religion!" *[See L. Ron Hubbard]*

With that, Farfalle stormed off, never to be seen again until the third gospel later on in the book.

As Bowtie went through the countryside preaching, he gathered together his A-team, fellow varieties of pasta, and called them the A-pastas. The first to join him was Vermicelli, and Vermicelli's brother Tortellini, also Capellini who was sometimes known as Angel Hair. Then there was Elbow, also called Macaroni, the favorite of Bowtie. Penne of Rigati too, and Rigatoni, who was whole-wheat, and a little sensitive about it as everyone else was of white flour. There joined him also Linguine, and Fettuccini, Manicotti, Ravioli, and Ravioli's sister Seashell, and lastly, Couscous, who was very small and not often heard when he spoke, and was sometimes mistaken for a grain.

The disciples of Bowtie amazed many people with various tricks of slight-of-hand, and impressive pick-up lines in all the clubs. And the people said, "Truly you are the son of the Flying Spaghetti Monster," but at other times they said: "I don't believe this guy is for real," because we have to account for Bowtie's being convincing enough for the reader to believe he is the Son of the FSM, and yet still explain why the people who actually knew him go ahead and kill him in the end. Even Bowtie's brothers who knew him better than anyone were not convinced that he was who he said he was, the anointed one (anointed with a delicious truffle olive oil) *[John 7:5]*. All of which is why it is all the more important that you believe based on One-Eyed Bill's second-hand story, because somebody has to believe all this if Bowtie's legacy is to carry any weight as a religion.

One day, Bowtie led his A-Pastas up a mountainside for dramatic effect, and all who had eyes to see, and ears to hear, knew that this was an important part of the story. And Bowtie asked each of them this:

"The mountain is rumbling and may soon spew hot lava and ash over the neighboring towns. How do we deal with it?"

"Well, the mountain is angry," Fettuccini offered, "and to appease it we should pray."

"It needs sacrifice," Vermicelli said. "We should sacrifice a bull."

"No, a human!" Tortellini interjected. "First born sons!"

"Easy for you to say, little brother," said Vermicelli.

"Virgins!" yelled Rigatoni.

"Whew! That leaves me out!" Manicotti said, not fooling anyone.

"KITTENS," said Couscous.

"You sick little bastard," said Seashell, who often worked weekends at the animal rescue shelter.

Bowtie shook his head, disappointed in them all. "You see, a volcano is what we call *'not alive.'*" He pointed to the steam rising out of the caldera at the top of the mountain. "It is not thinking it needs anything tossed into it. It is not thinking at all. It is not spewing lava and destroying towns because it wants something or is angry with anyone. It is spewing lava because there is a hot plume of magma under pressure and rising up from the mantle through the earth's crust as a result of thermodynamic convection and plate tectonics. You would know this if you had paid attention in science class."

"But what should we do, then?" asked Vermicelli.

"You should run away. Everyone should run away. You see, there is no reasoning with nature. It does what it does. You have attributed a sense of agency to the mountain, as though it is doing something for a purpose. You think of it as a living beast. You are not being stupid: it is quite natural that you made that mistake, for that is the natural way the human mind works, unless you are autistic. You see, our minds imagine minds in other things, whether they have minds or not. And we try to read intentions in that other mind. In fact, this is called *theory of mind*. We are more successful in our social maneuvering and interaction if we can model the minds of others. But in the case of this volcano, there is no agency, no intelligent mind behind its rumblings. And just like getting angry and yelling at a car that starts making funny noises does no good, our attempts to appease something that is not alive, such as this volcano, is quite ineffective. Instead, we need to understand the scientific model of its nature."

Bowtie let that sink in for a moment, as noodles are not known for great thinking capacity, which is surprising, this author thought in an aside, because we often refer to our brains as a *noodle*, although I do not know how common that term is among millennials. Bowtie waited for the author to get back on subject and reminded him that *noodle* is also slang for *penis*, and then continued: "Mankind has always assumed that things like rivers, storms, lightening, earthquakes, and the like, were alive, or moved by acts of gods, or were gods in the flesh. But we have figured out a lot of things over the past five hundred years. We understand plate tectonics, weather cycles, and lunar tides now. We know that coronal mass ejections from the sun cause auroras. We no longer see these things as the mystical actions of supernatural beings."

Just about this time, the clouds parted, and a long noodle descended and touched Bowtie on the shoulder. "This is my boy, Bowtie, in whom I am well pleased," boomed a gravelly voice, followed by a few hacking coughs.

"Holy shit!" cried Capellini. And even after seeing the noodley appendage of the Flying Spaghetti Monster himself and hearing a booming, unearthly voice call him his son, the A-pastas would all inexplicably express some degree of doubt in Bowtie's paternal claims later in our story when things get hairy.

Bowtie led his group down the mountain and out of harm's way of the eruption, which would begin any day now according to the scientific instruments placed by geologists near the top. No virgins were sacrificed, nor kittens. Science prevailed, though a few adventurous photographers were unfortunately buried in the ash and suffocated.

"So, all those people, and bulls, and kittens, and grain that have been sacrificed to appease the gods over the years were a waste of time, lives, and resources?" asked Fettuccini.

"Well, not a complete waste," Bowtie explained. "You see, it pulled people together for a united cause and fed a lot of priests over the years. But yes, it was quite inefficient, and the volcano erupted anyway if the magma was hot enough and the pressure high enough. Through the years, whenever the volcano did not blow up, the priests could point and say, 'See? It's working!' And the people bought into it and kept the fresh meat and donations coming. But when the volcano blew, they would say, '*You didn't pray hard enough*', or '*The brisket was a little tough.*'"

A few days later, as Bowtie and his A-pastas wandered through the countryside, Penne reprimanded Rigatoni for throwing his sandwich wrapper by the side of the road. "Littering is a sin!" Penne scolded.

"You are not my master!" Rigatoni snapped.

"What?" Penne was taken aback.

"You think you can tell me what to do because I'm whole-wheat," he said.

"Oh, my goodness, no!" Penne protested. "I am always after all you guys to pick up after yourselves. You know full well that I jumped all over Linguine the other day for sticking his gum on the telephone pole. It has nothing to do with you being whole-wheat. Besides, ..."

Rigatoni cut her off: "Don't say it! I know, some of your best friends are whole-wheat!"

"I was going to say there was a sign back there saying it's a 100-schmeckle fine for littering. So, pick up your damn wrapper."

Rigatoni didn't appreciate Penne's holier-than-thou attitude, but he bent down and picked up the wrapper anyway. "A sin? Where in the scriptures does it say that littering is a sin?" he asked her.

"Everyone knows littering is bad," insisted Penne. "Sin is bad. Litter is bad. Therefore, littering is a sin."

"Who can tell me the difference between sin and immoral behavior?" Bowtie asked, seizing the chance to impart a lesson.

After a few moments of shuffling feet and looking down so as not to be called upon by the teacher, Couscous finally spoke up: "Sin is dirtier?"

"No, my gentle, pea-brained Couscous. Sin is an offence against God, whereas immorality is an offense against your fellow man or woman."

"Or non-binary gender person," Linguine added. Vermicelli nodded.

"Is slavery a sin or immoral?" asked Bowtie.

"It is immoral, but not a sin, because the god Yahweh said we could take slaves from neighboring countries and even sell our daughters into slavery," said Tortellini, as he high-fived Ravioli. *[Exodus 21:7]*

"Very good, Tortellini," Bowtie said. "Whereas many god-forbidden acts like working on the Sabbath, or wearing cloth of mixed wool and linen, are sinful, but not immoral." *[Deuteronomy 22:11]*

"Wool and linen," Fettuccini shook his head. "Who would *do* that?"

"But what, then, is morality?" Bowtie asked.

Rigatoni offered: "Morality is knowing right from wrong. Doing good things is moral, and doing bad things is immoral."

"Okay," said Bowtie, "See, that doesn't help much. Does anyone know why?"

"Because retarded people can be good too, even if they don't know the difference?" Couscous asked. Bowtie did not have an answer to that.

When no one else spoke up, Bowtie continued: "It is because you haven't defined a system for determining what is right and what is wrong, or what is good and what is bad. We still don't know what makes something moral or immoral. We have no measuring stick, no moral compass to point the way."

"Being moral is behaving in a virtuous way," said Rigatoni. "We should always be loyal, obedient, dedicated, hard-working, truthful, cooperative, generous, and courteous."

Tortellini piped in: "And don't forget about going above and beyond the call of duty."

"Well, let's see," said Bowtie. He stopped and pointed to a scarecrow in the farmer's field they were passing by. "Manicotti, would you be so kind as to grab that scarecrow and post him over here?" Manicotti waded into the grain field to the straw man, yanked it up, and brought it back by the road. He poked its pole into the ground near the road, and everyone gathered around at the base of the scarecrow.

"Let's suppose that this is Dieter, a guard at Auschwitz," said Bowtie. He has all the virtues Rigatoni mentioned: he is fiercely loyal to Adolph Hitler. He's obedient to his camp commandant. He is dedicated, hard-working, truthful, and works in close cooperation with his fellow guards to ensure no one escapes and the work at hand gets done. He even donates generously to the Nazi widow's fund and buys his beloved anti-Semitic Aunt Hilde flowers once a month."

Ravioli reached into his pocket and pulled out a black armband with a swastika on a white circle. He walked up to the scarecrow and slipped it over his arm.

"Ravioli," Bowtie asked, "Where did you get that?"

"Somebody handed it to me at a Trump rally."

Bowtie gave him a stern look.

"What?" Ravioli wondered.

"Anyway, as I was saying, Dieter is a model guard at Auschwitz. His job is to process Jews through the gas chamber. He always politely invites the prisoners in as he stands by the air-lock door, making them feel welcome as best he can. He goes above and beyond the call of duty, and regularly exceeds the quotas his commandant sets, drawing praise from Berlin. You would never call him lazy or uncooperative. He works long hours, covering a shift for Hans, whose grandmother is in town for the week. He goes home late, and arrives early the next morning, because he is so dedicated to his job. Do all these virtues make him moral?"

Couscous stood up, walked over and kicked the scarecrow in the balls.

"Correct, Couscous," Bowtie said. "So, if admirable virtues do not make us moral, we are still stuck with the question: How do we know what *is* moral?"

"In college they taught us about Kant's Categorical Imperative, and John Stuart Mill's Utilitarianism, and John Rawls's social contract theory," said Penne. "I guess they are all ways of determining what is moral."

"Well, we could go over those ideas and put our readers to sleep," Bowtie acknowledged. "The truth is, a deep dive into Philosophy 101 and moral theory is mostly just academic masturbation. Fun for the geek, but not readily accessible by the average football fan. I imagine a stodgy old man sitting in an overstuffed chair by the fireplace in the library, a glass of port in hand, pondering whether evicting the widow Montgomery from her apartment would result in maximal human happiness."

Just then a dusty old farm truck came rumbling by. The driver slowed down to look at the A-Pastas sitting at the foot of a Nazi scarecrow, then quickly looked straight forward and sped up again.

"Well, when I want to do the right thing, I always just do what the *Supreme Creator of the Known Universe* ™ tells me to do," said Manicotti. "Doing His will is always the right thing to do. We should always be obedient to the big guy upstairs."

To which Bowtie replied: "But you are equating obedience to morality. If the *Supreme Creator of the Known Universe* told you to throw your sandwich wrappers on the road, would you do it?"

"Why yes!" said Manicotti. "It can only be for good yet mysterious reasons that he would ask me to do such a thing."

"If the *Supreme Creator of the Known Universe* told you to sacrifice your first-born, would you do it?"

"Well, ..." Manicotti paused. "I am sure he must have a good reason for it. Maybe my first-born would have grown up to be a serial killer?"

Now Manicotti was also called Rocky, because Bowtie compared him to a rock. "Thou art a rock," he said. "The question one might ask is why he would have you kill it, scarring you mentally, rather than just afflicting baby Charlie Manson with whooping cough?" Bowtie then asked: "What if the *Supreme Creator* told you to attack a city and kill every man, woman, child, and farm animal? Would you still do it?"

"Well, no," said Manicotti, "that is just freaking crazy and immoral."

"And yet we have examples of a god who supposedly did just that, and people who believed it was the right thing to do. Consider, also, when morality is defined by God, who is speaking for that God. It is the rare individual who gets the '*divine*' message firsthand, and when they claim to have received the divine word directly, it is impossible for anyone else to verify that claim. And if God is that fatherly voice in your head telling you the *right* thing to do, listen again: it is your own voice. If you don't believe me, just have that deep voice of wisdom tell you the joke about the Rabbi and the Pirate who walk into a bar. There really is no way to distinguish between your imagination, aural hallucination, and a genuine disembodied voice in your head. If you honestly hear voices and you can't control them, you should seek professional help rather than act on what they are telling you to do." *(Google the cases of Laurel Schlemmer and Deanna Laney for two examples.)*

"But how then will we know right from wrong?" Linguine asked.

"Here is where I think most of the philosophers get things backwards," Bowtie explained. "Things are right or wrong for a number of reasons, morality being just one aspect of it, though probably the most important consideration. Other things we must consider include legality, economics, social norms, civil duties, previous agreements, reputation, personal consequences, personal survival, and self-interest, all of which are not necessarily moral aspects but impact the rightness or wrongness of an action as far as it concerns us. So, the question is not what is right or wrong, but what is the moral aspect of determining right or wrong?"

Then Elbow Macaroni spoke up, saying: "Morality is the golden rule: Do unto others as you would have others do unto you." *(And this is why oral sex is considered the highest virtue among the break-off sect of followers of Elbow today.)*

"Yes, thank you, Elbow," said Bowtie. "You are getting closer. But by that logic, if I need my mother-in-law bumped off, and you need yours likewise, we can do it for each other. Yet somehow it does not seem very moral."

Elbow smiled and nodded absent-mindedly, as he was still thinking about the oral-sex thing. *(And so were you. Admit it.)*

"Here is the point I am trying to make." The A-pastas leaned forward, for they sensed that great wisdom was coming. "Morality," said Bowtie, "is the breadth and degree to which we extend kindness, compassion, dignity, equality, fairness, and justice to others."

"THAT'S IT?" said Couscous.

"And the other side of the coin is Immorality," Bowtie continued, "which is the degree to which we unfairly seek gain to the disadvantage of others, oppress or disparage others, or take pleasure in the pain or misfortune of others."

"And you are saying we should always choose the moral option over the immoral option?" Penne asked.

"I am saying that this should be the foundation of your moral compass. Given a choice, you should consider doing what is more moral than less moral, and you should always avoid that which is immoral."

"But why? Dostoevsky said *without God anything is permitted*! Sounds like we can do whatever we want," Fettuccini said.

"That is what we call a non-sequitur. It does not follow that anything is permitted if there is no God to say what is okay. Society permits or prohibits. Your conscience permits or prohibits. We live by rules because it is the logical choice. Given a choice to live in a compassionate world where everyone is kind and fair, or a merciless world where everyone is out for themselves and winner take all, which would you choose?"

"NICE PEOPLE!" yelled Couscous.

"Thank you, Couscous. And that is all the logic and reason we need to live morally."

There was a nodding of heads, and Bowtie continued:

"The point is not that we must always choose the *most* moral action, but that we should aim higher on the morality scale than we normally would, based on our evolved moral sentiments. And to clearly understand morality, we should not muddle it together with obedience, duty, social norms, or loyalty. These things are only moral issues when they affect how we practice kindness, compassion, respect, or fairness. And it is not black and white. We often cannot draw a line between what is moral and what is immoral, but we can usually say what is more moral or less moral."

"So that is your scientific theory of Morality?" Tortellini asked.

"No," Bowtie explained, "That is my philosophy. A *theory* starts with observations. We observe moral sentiments, which are what we feel, and from that we develop a theory to explain why we feel what we feel. We could point to the evolutionary benefits of kin-favoritism in certain moral sentiments, for example. A moral theory is meant to describe and model *what is*. But a moral *philosophy* is a proposed way of guiding our moral reasoning. A philosophy describes *what ought to be*."

The A-pastas were silent for a moment, wrapping their noodles around this.

"Common moral sentiments emerged in man, an extension of what we would call a moral code among our primate ancestors. We feel empathy, sympathy, and compassion. We have a strong sense of fairness when we are on the receiving end of injustice. We act in ways to ensure propagation of our own genes, so we favor kin and people who look like us. And the more distantly related others are, or the stranger they look or dress or speak, the less compassion and empathy we tend to hold for them. As we overpopulate and the inevitable competition for resources begins, we will always ally with kin against those who are not kin. But as a rational, morally cognizant species, I propose that we *ought* to extend our moral consideration to all people."

"But doesn't your idea of being kind to everyone run counter to the way evolution has molded us?" Fettuccini asked.

"Exactly," said Bowtie. "We need to seek a higher morality, higher than what results from the evolutionary process, and closer to the ideals expressed but not well practiced by many of the world's religions: *do unto others*, and *Peace on Earth, Goodwill toward Man*. The idea that all people are created equal. Not as a commandment, but as a logical means of making this a better world, because we all want to live in a better world. But it is an *unnatural* morality, and it takes work. It takes a little more objectivity in our judgment rather than just reacting to our feelings. The important thing is that you can use this framework, the idea of extending equality, respect, compassion, fairness, and dignity to all people, and to some degree to all species that feel pain and fear, to critically think about the morality of anything. And the moral scale applies across all time and cultures. We cannot say that something was once moral in some other place and time but isn't now. If it is immoral here and now, it always was."

"I'm not so sure," said doubting Tortellini. "If it's objective, why is there so much moral disagreement?"

"You will always have disagreement because you will always have different values," Bowtie answered. "Some things are clearly moral, and other things are clearly immoral. But there is a wide gray area where it depends how we weight our values. America was founded on two basic principles: freedom and equality. But these two ideals conflict with each other, especially where it involves some form of redistribution of wealth. Do we respect the right of the individual to keep what they have worked hard for, or do we ensure that everyone has equal access to health and education? You have the far-left communists and socialists requiring the complete redistribution of wealth on the one hand, and the libertarian who wants no taxation and an unregulated capitalist free-market on the other. The only thing most people can agree upon is that the extreme ends of the spectrum are really bad. Communism kills any incentive to work, but Karl Marx wrote the Communist Manifesto in response to the horrible social inequity in the 1840's that resulted from unbridled capitalism."

"That still doesn't answer the moral dilemmas we studied in college. How do we know the right thing to do?" Rigatoni asked. "If I am standing by the switch, and a runaway trolley is hurtling down the tracks toward a cute chick, should I throw the switch and direct it onto the track where fifty accident lawyers are standing? Or should I push a fat lawyer in front of the trolley? How do I know what is moral?"

"That, my son, is merely a calculation," Bowtie answered. "We don't mind switching the tracks, but we would prefer the fat guy make his own choice to give his life to save others. And we don't call them *chicks* anymore. They are now empowered young ladies of equal status. The main thing is that you feel concern for people who are about to be killed and maimed. If the decision is a dilemma for you, you are a good person.

The answer, by the way, is to throw the switch and save the cute chick. Otherwise the fifty lawyers will sue you for her death."

There was some puzzling and head scratching among the group. "But what about all the other immoral stuff?" Fettuccini asked. "Isn't sex dirty and immoral?"

"And I was always taught that homosexuality was immoral," Linguine said. "Aren't homosexuals bad, sinful people?"

"Good question, Linguine. What any two consenting people do with each other's genitalia is their own business. All we are to do is to extend to all people, of whatever sex, gender identity, or sexual orientation, the same kindness, compassion, dignity, fairness, and equality we do for anyone else. Various religions have condemned homosexuality as a sin against God and conflated that into immorality."

"But homosexuality is not natural! You don't see it in nature," Elbow said.

"We see it all the time in nature. The Christian Right will repeat that claim over and over again, but when we study bonobos, dolphins, birds, dogs, and quite a few other animals, we see homosexuality all the time. It's so frequent that it must be accepted as the natural state of affairs that some percentage of any population of any given species will be so inclined."

"But if sex is not evil, why do I feel so dirty?" asked Manicotti. "For truly when I look with lust upon the beautiful lady noodles, do I not sin?"

"You have issues, Manicotti," said Bowtie. "It is human nature to have and enjoy sex. Just remember the cardinal rule of sex: the other person has to give consent. 'No' means no, stop right there. Rape is wrong, as is pressuring someone into doing what they don't want to do. Keep it in your pants and don't force yourself on anyone else. Especially, don't prey upon those not yet of the age of consent. Practice safe sex, avoid unwanted pregnancy with contraceptives, be respectful and discreet, and if you have agreed to a monogamous relationship, keep your promise. It is the betrayal that is immoral. And if you make a baby, step up to the plate. Every kid needs a parent, and two is better than one."

"What about masturbation? Is that bad?" asked Couscous.

"Whack away, Couscous," Bowtie said.

"NOW?" said Couscous.

"Do not confuse morality with decency, my little one," said Bowtie. "Whipping one's penis out in public may not be immoral, but it is certainly indecent in the present society. For morality is universal, but decency falls within the social context. You may walk around buck naked amongst the bushmen of the Kalahari and no one will bat an eye. But do the same in Cleveland and you will be arrested."

"Yes," Elbow added, "You may wear a Speedo on the beach, but not to a wedding, unless the wedding is on the beach and the invitation clearly stated *informal attire*. Believe me, I know."

Now sex was on the mind of all the noodles, so Bowtie tried to distract them by talking about baseball. The discussion quickly turned to great ball players and their hot wives, and soon everyone was back to talking about sex again.

"I'm still a little confused," said Penne. "Did we decide if littering is a sin?"

"Littering would seem to fall into the category of offenses against your fellow human being," Bowtie explained. "But I would categorize it as thoughtless rather than immoral. Nobody likes to see litter along a road, especially one so pretty as this. And we should always try to recycle and not fill our landfills so quickly. Sometimes morality comes in the form of kindness to people in the future, people we don't even know."

Now there was a wedding a few days later for some friends of Seashell which Bowtie was asked to officiate, and the A-pastas were all invited. What Bowtie liked best about these affairs was that he could get away without putting on a tie and he still looked dressed up. He did wear a cummerbund, though.

When the family and friends had all gathered, Bowtie conducted the wedding with these words:

"Dear friends and family, we are gathered here today to join Terry and Pat in marriage, a legal status which may help your tax situation, yes, but marriage is much more than that. You see, there is no nebulous 'institution' of marriage. There is no magical bond of divine blessing that descends over you. Marriage is between two people. It does not matter what anyone else thinks of your marriage, or how they might define marriage. There is nobody in this marriage but you two, Pat and Terry. It is as beautiful and special as you want it to be."

Bowtie picked up a bottle of wine from the small table before him and poured it into a beautiful crystal goblet.

"Marriage is not a thing that you create and put on a shelf to admire now and then. It is something you *do* and will be doing for the rest of your lives together. It is up to you to make your marriage work, and to keep it a special bond between yourselves. It's not going to be easy. Try not to kill each other. That is why we have divorce. But love brought you both here today, and it is that love which you should strive to keep alive. The beginning is easy, with the excitement of novelty and passion. And the final golden years are easy, full of love, shared memories, and the comfort of companionship. It is all those years in the middle that will challenge you."

Bowtie paused and took a sip of the wine, which Pat thought was meant for them to seal the deal at the end of the ceremony, but apparently Bowtie was just thirsty.

Wiping his mouth on his sleeve, Bowtie continued: "Take comfort in your marriage, but not so much that you take each other for granted. Bathe regularly and practice good oral hygiene, and every now and then pretend it is your first date and you are out to win the other's heart again."

Turning toward those in attendance, Bowtie said: "If anyone here knows of a reason why these two should not be joined in marriage, please keep it to yourself and carry it to the grave, unless you have evidence that they were siblings separated in early childhood."

After a brief pause in which no one spoke up, Bowtie held up the two rings and said: "A ring is a circle of precious metal with a hole in the middle. You stick your finger through the hole."

Couscous snickered until someone swatted him on the head.

"This symbolizes the journey you are making together, each entering into the life of the other. It encircles you, enriches you, binds you."

"Do you, Pat, take Terry as your spouse and equal, with whom you will share love, respect, chores, laughter, and all things, in good times and bad, in sickness and in health?"

"You bet I do," said Pat.

Vermicelli blew his nose at this point, and Fettuccini tried to make fun of him for crying, but his eyes were welling up too.

"And do you, Terry, take Pat as your spouse and equal, with whom you will share love, respect, chores, laughter, and all things, in good times and bad, in sickness and in health?"

"I sure do," said Terry.

"By the power vested in me by Pat and Terry, who are the only two who can really declare this a marriage, I now pronounce you spouse and spouse. You may kiss each other tastefully without too much tongue."

Terry and Pat kissed, and it was beautiful and romantic regardless of how this scene plays out in the mind of the reader.

"Remember the promise you have made to each other today," Bowtie said. "Try not to screw it up."

And then the party started.

At the reception, some of the guests slipped out back to smoke a joint, but it quickly ran out, as each of the six partakers only got a brief toke before Vermicelli bogarted the doobie. Bowtie saw this and pointed to the marijuana plant in the back yard. "A miracle!" they cried, and then proceeded to roll and smoke until all were stoned. This caused a stir among the later followers of Bowtie, for some said he was in favor of pot, while others said he was not, and each could find verses in this gospel to support their stand. But unlike many ancient scriptures which leave stuff like this open to debate, I, One-Eyed Bill, will clarify this here.

Bowtie was firmly in favor of the legalization of cannabis, as its occasional use in private harmed no one but the user, and its prohibition did more damage than good, just as prohibition of alcohol caused more problems than simply promoting responsible drinking. "For like any drug such as alcohol and nicotine," said Bowtie, "when its use harms others, especially in the case of driving under the influence, it is a moral issue. But when it harms only the user, it is a lifestyle choice." But Bowtie also advised: "Life is too short to waste it with a muddled brain and an unhealthy body. There is substantial indication that pot smoking during the teens and early twenties causes lasting brain damage, limited achievement, and reduction in intelligence. New breeds of marijuana contain much more THC than it did years ago. One should always value bodily health and clarity of the mind."

A while later, Bowtie found Capellini in the parlor, sitting cross-legged on the floor with a young lady. "Ah, Bowtie," said Capellini, "I want you to meet Moonbeam." He gestured toward the woman sitting opposite him who smiled and said hello. She had big, round glasses perched on her nose, and wore her hair in long braids. "She has been helping me get my chakras in line. I didn't even know I had any!"

"Oh, silly," Moonbeam laughed. "You just haven't been in touch with yourself."

"OH YES HE HAS!" said Couscous.

"Chakras are where the energy meridians in your body intersect," she explained to Bowtie. "There are seven main ones, so I am showing Capellini how to find them and get their energy flowing again."

"She has been vibrating mine with this crystal," Capellini added, pointing to the polished quartz on the floor between them. "It works like a tuning fork. You have two chakras in your head, and one in your throat, your chest, your abdomen, your hips, and your butt."

"I see she gets your lower ones humming," said Bowtie.

"The crystal also improves your psychic abilities, so we can connect at a deeper level," Moonbeam explained. "I am sensing a blockage of energy right here." She pointed at his heart. "This piece of jade will fix that," she said as she reached over with a green stone and rubbed it over his chest. "You like that?"

"Oh, yeah baby, I like that," Capellini said.

Bowtie cleared his throat. "You know, this would all make a lot of sense if there were some corresponding anatomical structure that matched up to what you are describing here, Moonbeam. And in a way, there is. We have a brain, and a spinal column, and a nervous system that we can trace. Every inch of our bodies is lined with nerves radiating out from the spinal column. Energy does flow through the body in the form of carbohydrates, from the digestive track through our blood vessels to our cells where mechanisms in the cells use the action of glucose oxidation to generate molecules of ATP which act as biological batteries. I don't doubt that meditation and imagining the flow of energy through these areas will make you relax and feel better. The placebo effect is very strong in some people. But what matters is ensuring you have good blood circulation and a healthy musculoskeletal structure through exercise, stretching, and mental relaxation practices. The fact is, those crystals are not vibrating anything. It's all in your head. I hope you did not pay too much for the magic stones."

Moonbeam smiled and said: "Ah, a skeptic. Some people only believe things that you can prove."

"Yes, that would be me," Bowtie confirmed. "The alternative is gullibility, or at best, living in a fantasy world."

"You think everything has to be measured and tested before you can accept it. But you have to see with your heart if you are to understand the mysteries of the world," she said.

"Seeing with the heart is good for feeling empathy and compassion, but it's not understanding. It is only *imagining* that you understand. People believe a lot of things that they feel in their hearts that is either demonstrably false or completely unverifiable. When you talk about crystals stimulating one's chakras, you are making a testable claim about the physical world. The only way of knowing what is real and what is not is by measuring and testing. All else is conjecture, and often just imaginary. When you can show me an impartial double-blinded study on the measurable efficacy of crystals for a specific health condition that exceeds the placebo effect, I will be glad to take it seriously."

"There are lots of things you feel but can't measure. Don't you feel love? It's not measurable. Are you saying love does not exist?" said Moonbeam.

"I do feel love," replied Bowtie. "It exists as an electro-chemical stimulation in the brain. Emotions are brain states which affect our experience in the world, but the experience itself does not extend beyond the mind, much like imagination. In the case of crystals, you are describing a physical phenomenon external to a concept in the mind, and so it should be measurable. If crystals actually sent vibrations through the air and stimulated energy centers in the body, this would be detectable and could be scientifically studied."

Moonbeam stood up and gathered her magic stones. "I can see I am wasting my time with you," she said, and walked away.

"Thanks a lot, Bowtie," said Capellini. "I bet you don't get laid very often."

The A-pastas wandered throughout the region preaching great things to the Pastafarians and distributing eye patches. But they occasionally passed through towns where goombahs lived, for *goombah* was the slightly offensive term reserved for anyone who was not a Pastafarian. And when a young goombah woman asked Elbow about this great wisdom, and would he share it with her, though she was not a Pastafarian, he quoted Matthew 15:21: "It is not good to take bread from the children and toss it to the dogs."

"Are you comparing me to a dog?" she asked, a bit miffed.

"Um, yeah," Elbow thought. "But even dogs get to eat scraps under the table. So, I will throw you a bone of wisdom: Don't play the slot machines."

And after the young woman stormed off in anger, Bowtie came unto Elbow and said: "Elbow, be not a jerk. Dividing the world into Pastafarians and Goombahs serves only to create an us-versus-them mentality."

"But we can't preach to the goombahs until they first convert to Pastafarianism. They must accept the eyepatch," Elbow protested.

"No, Elbow! Don't you see?" Manicotti jumped in, "Bowtie is the new covenant! We don't need no stinking eyepatches anymore. Bowtie dies in a really nasty way, and everybody gets to cash in on it. Then it will be us Bowtians against the Pastafarians who reject Bowtie's gracious sacrifice." Bowtie began to look a little uncomfortable at this suggestion. "Go on, tell him, Bowtie! Tell Elbow we don't need to follow the old rules."

"Well, I don't think I said we should just abandon *all* the old rules. Things like not killing each other and not stealing are pretty good policies, and we should keep our thirty-day guarantee that dissatisfied followers can go back to their old god with no questions asked. But no, I don't see why they need to wear an eyepatch to live a good life."

"But goombahs are dirty. They fornicate, and sacrifice children, and eat shellfish," said Elbow.

Bowtie looked at him sideways. "Really? Child sacrifice?"

"Well, they do eat shellfish."

"You know how I feel about clam sauce," interrupted Linguine.

"Stop calling them *Goombahs*. You are creating an artificial divide, separating *us* from *them*. When you look at others, I want you to see yourself in them. What did I say about morality?" Bowtie asked. The A-pastas all remained silent, for none of them could remember.

"Come, now, this is possibly the most important thing I taught you." But the silence continued.

"Jesus," Bowtie muttered to himself, rolling his eyes. He took a deep breath and said: "Morality is the breadth and degree to which we extend kindness, compassion, dignity, equality, fairness, and justice to others." He paused, then added: "*All* others, and even other sentient species."

The A-pastas bowed their heads in shame, for they realized they had been daydreaming a few pages back.

As they neared Rome *[some texts say Trenton]*, the A-Pastas learned of a political rally to protest a new law that forbade transgender people from using public restrooms. In those days it was commonly said throughout the land (this being passive voice but we know full well it was the religious conservatives who said it) that transgender people are just using their transgender status to get into a bathroom to molest little children, although it was extremely hard to find a case where this had ever happened, and there was no evidence that transgender people had any higher rates of pedophilia than the rest of the population. Bowtie suggested that they should attend the rally and stand up for the rights of their LGBT brethren, sisteren, and non-binary genderen.

"But Bowtie," said Manicotti, "Why do you care? Your rights aren't being infringed!"

"My dear Manicotti," Bowtie frowned. "Let me tell you a story. When my uncle Gnocchi was a little boy in Poland, the Nazis invaded. One afternoon, his mother burst into the workshop where my uncle was helping his father repair shoes. His mother, out of breath, cried: "Papa, the Nazi's are taking away the homosexuals and putting them in a concentration camp!"

Papa replied: "Don't worry. We are not gay." He turned back to his shoes.

Two days later, Mama came running up to Papa in the meadow, saying: "Papa, they are taking away the Jews!"

"We are not Jewish. Relax, Mama. We have nothing to fear," Papa said.

A few days later, Mama burst into the kitchen to find Papa sitting at the table smoking his pipe. "Papa, the Nazis are confiscating noodles to feed the troops!"

"Now they have gone too far!" said Papa. "We must do something."

So, Bowtie spoke at the rally, telling this story all over again, and earned many new friends and Twitter followers, and word went out into the land of this pasta who said such amazing things.

Soon, a mob of Pastafarians and Evangelicals began to form, for the people were quite concerned about this preacher who taught reason and thinking rather than blind faith and eyepatches. The A-pastas began to be afraid and started second guessing Bowtie.

That night, as they dined at the Olive Garden on Gethsemane Street, Doubting Tortellini asked: "How will we know you are truly the one, the son of the Flying Spaghetti Monster?"

"If, after I am dead and eaten," Bowtie explained, taking another scoop of bottomless salad, "and then you see me risen, then you will know that I am not the one, and Jesus is real." And they all looked at him in amazement.

"But if you see me ascend into the sky on a flying horse, then you will know that Muhammed is the last and greatest prophet of God." And they were even more amazed.

"And if the angel Moroni appears and tells you to fear not, then know that Joseph Smith is really the greatest prophet of God." They were a little less amazed at this.

"And if I am reincarnated as a baby noodle, then the Buddha had it right." They all nodded politely, and some began to check their text messages.

"But if I stay dead, if I am unrisen, then you will know that I am the one, the true son of the Flying Spaghetti Monster, for I will be dead and gone, just as I have said."

The A-pastas were amazed again and put their phones back in their pockets.

"Truly you are the anointed one," Manicotti finally broke the silence, "I will follow you to the ends of the earth. I pledge my whole life to you and am willing to die for you."

"ME TOO! Except the *die* part," said Couscous.

Bowtie set down his Mai Tai and said: "Verily, I say unto you, Manicotti, that before the parrot squawks thrice, you will deny me to save yourself."

"Never, my lord!" Manicotti protested.

"Don't call me *lord*. It sounds so feudal," Bowtie chastised him. "Oh, ye of little faith, I grow weary of you. Some rock of the church you are." Bowtie knew the time of his demise was drawing near, and began to babble a bit, trying to make sure he got everything important across to his team.

"There will be many false noodles who will come," he said.

"The impastas!" yelled Fettuccini.

"So, you must be vigilant and get the sanctioned word of the Flying Spaghetti Monster out to the people. Let me summarize all I have taught you, so you can clearly explain it to everyone after I am gone."

Now some of the A-pastas were nodding off, their bellies full of the baked spaghetti special. *[Scholars are in general agreement that the cannibalistic implication of this passage was purely for comic relief.]*

"Wake up! I can't believe you guys are sleeping!" Bowtie said in exasperation. "It's all very simple. I say unto all of you, if you are to follow me, you must hate your parents *[Luke 14:26]*. For I have come to turn a man against his father, a daughter against her mother *[Matt 10:35]*."

"And that does NOT sound like some mentally abusive cult leader trying to isolate his followers," Linguine piped in.

Bowtie gave Linguine the stink-eye, and then continued: "And love everyone, even your enemies *[Matt 5:44]*. If someone slaps you on the right cheek, turn and offer the left *[Luke 6:29]*. But remember I did not come to bring peace, but a sword *[Matt 10:34]*. And if you don't have a sword, sell your colander and buy one *[Luke 22:36]*."

Linguine drew out his samurai sword that he found online for an incredible price. It was made in Korea, and while it was sharp, he had been a bit disappointed when the wrapping on the hilt had started to unwind.

"Concerning modesty," Bowtie said, "Let your light shine before men so that they may see your good deeds *[Matt 5:16]*. But take care not to do your good deeds in public to be seen by men *[Matt 6:1]*."

And if that was not confusing enough, he went on to say: "I am the way, the truth and the life *[John 14:6]*, the son of the Flying Spaghetti Monster, but if I testify about myself, my testimony is not true *[John 5:31]*."

At this the A-pastas began to murmur amongst themselves, because while they had heard Bowtie say all these things before, hearing them juxtaposed next to each other was a bit confusing.

"No, seriously, now that I think about it, the things I just said are kind of bat-shit crazy. How about everyone just be nice to each other, do good things, and enjoy your families. Obviously, protect yourself and others when you need too, but everyone should mellow out and get along. Put away that stupid sword, Linguine. You're going to hurt someone with it."

On the eve of the Feast of Pizza, the narrator's favorite feast by the way, Bowtie led the A-pastas into Rome *[or Trenton]* to preach the good news.

But the Pastafarians objected to Bowtie's break with the eyepatch, even though it's use has been associated to a significant increase in auto accidents among people with full eyesight. In response, they formed the Committee for Religiously Arbitrary Elucidations (CRAE). A sect of the Pastafarians, the Craft Brewers Guild, became concerned when Bowtie questioned the reality of beer volcanoes in Heaven, and rallied together the Citizens for Righteous Alcohol Enjoyment (also CRAE).

Additionally, when conservative Christians learned of Bowtie's teachings which permitted people to enjoy their bodies and accept scientifically sound ideas regardless of the religious implications, they soon organized the Angry Protestant-Evangelical Society for Hindering Innovative Thinking (APESHIT) in protest.

Seeing how the people had gone all APESHIT and CRAE-CRAE, Bowtie appealed for calm: "Chill, people! For you all take yourselves too seriously."

An old pirate standing at the back of the crowd, with a parrot on his shoulder, spat on the ground. The parrot squawked loudly: "Awwk! Blow the man down!"

Bowtie said unto them who were there: "You must eat of my flesh, and drink of my tomato sauce, for I am the food of life." But he carried this metaphor a bit too far, and the people began to look at him with hunger. "Really," he said, "Eat me." The crowd began to get a little unruly and quickly found a large pot and gathered firewood and soon had it lit in ravenous anticipation. The head of the angry evangelicals called out to seize Bowtie, for Bowtie spoke such blasphemies, and looked so delicious.

"Please, Bowtie, I beseech thee! Run for it!" said Manicotti. "For even though I know you are the chosen one, and I have seen you perform miracles and raise people from the dead, and I've seen your head glow with divine light as the noodly appendage descended from the clouds to touch you, and I've seen you talking with the pirate ghosts of yore, and in spite of the fact that you are the most important person in history, we need to get the hell out of here."

But Bowtie stood fast.

Two guards came forward to grab Bowtie. "Run, Bowtie!" said Linguine, seizing the opportunity to put his Korean sword to use as he cut the ear off one of the guards, who would not press charges because he was an insignificant character in the story.

Again, the parrot on the pirate's shoulder squawked: "Awwk! It's the plank fer ye."

Now what happened before the quickly assembled Court of the Pointy Finger is recorded for all to wonder at. When the head finger pointer asked Bowtie if he was indeed the son of the FSM, Bowtie tried to play coy, and said: "So you say," which might have left room for the finger pointers to let things slide.

"Good job, Bowtie," Rigatoni said to himself. "Keep it vague. Don't give them the rope to hang you," he thought.

But then Bowtie suddenly blurted out: "I am the son of the Flying Spaghetti Monster, and you shall see me coming like a Friday night entrée special, covered in sauce and sitting at the right-hand side of the breadsticks." At this the entire court gasped and screamed blasphemy, for breadsticks are always served ahead of time and not brought as a side with the entrée.

"Jeesh! That was not cool," Rigatoni muttered to himself.

"Boil him!" the people screamed.

And they did place the large pot of water on the fire, and the water began to boil.

"Didn't I see you with Bowtie earlier," a hungry little girl in the back of the crowd asked Manicotti as the steam began to rise, perhaps thinking there was room in that pot for one more.

"Never saw him before in my life," Manicotti said.

And immediately the parrot on the pirate's shoulder squawked a third time: "Awwk! Manicotti's a faithless bastard."

Manicotti bowed his head in shame, remembering what Bowtie had foretold.

And as the water vigorously boiled with a little salt and olive oil added in to keep the noodles from sticking together, the head angry person asked Bowtie if he repented from his common sense.

"And if I said 'yes', would I have to listen to your sermon again about how the Almighty will burn us in eternal Hell if we don't accept his gracious forgiveness and love?"

"Of course. That's what I do."

"Eat me."

Thus, with a whole lot of disturbing screaming, Bowtie was plunged into the boiling water. Once the screaming stopped, they boiled him for nine minutes, and then scooped him into the colander to drain, poured on the tomato sauce, sprinkled some grated parmesan over the top, and proceeded to devour him.

Though there was a rumor that Bowtie was seen the following weekend in a bar in Naples *[some texts say Newark]*, this was just hearsay started by the authorities to make people think that Bowtie was risen.

Three days later, there being no sign of Bowtie, Seashell announced that, just as Bowtie had predicted, he was unrisen.

"Well, you can't argue with prophecy," Linguine said. "Especially when it is free of any testable verification and is fulfilled in the same text as it was predicted, without any other independent contemporary corroborating accounts."

And the A-pastas went out into the countryside to proclaim the good news of the unrisen Bowtie. To this day, no one has seen him since.

The Gospel of Newt

Come and listen to a story 'bout a mate named Newt.
Poor buccaneer had plundered hardly any loot.
Then one day when he was feeling kind of sad,
Along came a noodle with a message from his dad.
Bowtie, that is.
Divine pasta, Holy guy.

[Millennials: see Beverly Hillbilllies theme song]

T'were a foggy winter evening, and I, Newt, had taken a room at the Green Parrot. I was biding me time between adventures on the high seas as I awaited me captain and crew of buccaneers to get back from shore leave. I was looking for a game of pinochle the night I met the son of the Flying Spaghetti Monster, and me life was changed forever, or at least for the next couple of months.

Now mind ye, I was a pirate, but I had been a good, God-fearin pirate. I always said me prayers before digging into me food, or me harlots, and I don't mind sayin that out there on the stormy seas I pooped meself more than once and promised God I would be a good man if He would only get me safely back to port. But you see, I had recently lost me faith. Sure and it was all mostly smooth sailing, marauding through the week, and church on Sundays. Lousy music but good potlucks, and more than a few pretty young wenches in the pews.

But then one day, after we raided a ship bound for Boston, full of MIT types it were, I came across several books amongst the booty, including a copy of Charles Darwin's *Origin of the Species*, Murray Gell-Mann's *The Quark and the Jaguar*, and a tattered edition of Stephen Hawking's *A Brief History of Time*. I read them all, bein' rather hungry as I was for some academic material which is often hard to come by on a pirate ship. Mostly all we had laying around were *Hardy Boys* mysteries, and Robert, the ship's cook, had a few *Nancy Drews* which he didn't like to share since they usually came back a bit messed up.

By the time we returned to port, it all clicked. It dawned on me that we didn't need to have gods to explain the world and everything in it. The amazing diversity we see is best explained by understanding the simple processes that give rise to ever-increasing levels of complexity. Everything made sense now: we don't need to imagine an even more complex creator to explain it all. And if there was no deity providing oversight as I had always been taught, then the age-old philosophical problem of Evil disappears. How can there be a benevolent, all powerful god, and yet Evil exists? The answer was that there wasn't any benevolent, all powerful god. There was just Evil. And Good of course, but all mixed together, because shit and shinola both happen (*See the author's thesis*). This would explain why we have malaria and sickle cell anemia, why so many little children starve each day, and why Carmen Electra married Dennis Rodman. There was simply no divine justice. *[Millennials: substitute Kim Kardashian and Kanye West.]*

But it hit me like a spinnaker in a gale. Me life had been built on belief in a higher cause and the promise of an afterlife. Without God there could be no meaning, I thought. If life be temporary, what be the point? If there be no law giver, there be no law, and if there be no purpose giver, there be no purpose.

So that night I sipped me rum and looked around at the sad faces in the bar. A young couple on a date occupied a near table. The boy was nodding with a dull smile as his date described in detail her conversation with her roommate the day before about a stain the roommate had gotten on the skirt she had borrowed. Three old salty dogs stared into their beers at the other end of the bar, none of them willing to bring up yet another fish story. They smelled of squid, even from where I was sitting.

I was drinking away me existential doom and gloom. I had lost me compass. Me lighthouse had gone dark. I was a ship without a rudder. Without God I figured anything goes, including overused nautical metaphors. No rules for the likes of me. Or 'twere until I met Bowtie and learned of the Flying Spaghetti Monster.

T'were early evening when the A-pastas took a room at the inn, and the twelve and their leader came down to the bar to order a round of drinks. A bit disappointed they were, as the barkeep knew not what went into a gimlet. "Save yer breath, me hearties," I said. "Thar's naught but rum and Dos Equis here." I dragged a chair over to strike up a conversation. "Ahoy, mates! Might ye fancy a game of pinochle?" Bein' strangers in town, they were eager to take up me offer of cards and companionship, and soon we were gathered round and dealing the first hand as the innkeeper brought out the roast beef sandwiches and clam chowder.

"Me name be Newt. Pleased to meet ye," I said as the one called Vermicelli shuffled. "Can't say as I've ever met a gang of pasta before. What brings ye to Kingston?"

"I am Bowtie, the son of the Flying Spaghetti Monster," declared Bowtie. "I've come to spread the good news of critical thinking, rigorous science, and healthy skepticism."

"We seek the enlightenment of others," Fettuccini explained, "So that we might bring a bit more common sense into the world."

"Cause when people talk stupid, it is SO ANNOYING!" said the little guy, Couscous.

I shot him the squinty eye, but he just smiled back at me. "Enlightenment, eh? I guess we could all use some enlightenment," I said.

"You see, the only thing for certain in this world is the Flying Spaghetti Monster," said Vermicelli. "Everything else needs to be challenged. We need to scrutinize everything we have ever been told if we are to arrive at the truth, or at least the closest possible approximation to the truth."

"The FSM? Why it just so happens that I have lost me faith in me previous god, so I am in the market for a new deity," I said with a sigh. "It's not easy giving up a god. Jehovah's going to burn me in Hell for eternity for not believing in him."

"For eternity? That's a long time," Bowtie observed.

"Perhaps the longest," I said. "What could be worse than being cast in a horrible lake of fire. Boiling, boiling, boiling. Can you imagine?"

"Tell me about it," Bowtie sympathized.

"What will the Flying Spaghetti Monster do to me if I don't believe in him?"

"Nothing at all. He's not vindictive. What kind of a sadistic bastard would burn you in Hell for not believing something without evidence? Or even *with* it for that matter."

"Well, at least Jehovah gave me some sort of purpose I suppose."

"And what would that be?" Bowtie asked me.

"To sing his praises," I explained. "The big guy can't seem to get enough of it."

"Yet I don't understand how that gives you much of a purpose. You are just one of thousands, millions even, singing to an egotistical god with self-esteem issues. But I have a sneaking suspicion that the boiling lake of fire is all made up to scare you into professing belief. Perhaps the world is ruled by an invisible, benevolent flying spaghetti monster rather than an insanely jealous and sadistic desert storm god. How would we know the difference? What if there are no gods, no heaven or hell? What if all this religion stuff is made up? With so many different versions, it seems like it is all more a work of imagination than of revelation."

"So, ye don't think any of this revealed divine knowledge stuff is real?" I asked.

Bowtie looked down a moment in thought. "Okay, if divine revelation is a real thing, that would make four kinds of people who claim to hear the voice of God in their heads: psychotics, the delusional hyper-religious, self-serving false prophets, and finally, real prophets."

"Aye. And so how would ye suss out the real prophets?"

"We know there are the first three types. Psychosis is a symptom which arises from a variety of mental illnesses, substance abuse, or damage to the temporal lobe, which often manifests itself in the form of disembodied voices speaking to the sufferer. As for the second type, many people in hyper-religious households are raised to believe that the little voice inside their head is God speaking to them. Actually, it's the same internal thoughts and moral conscientiousness we all have going on inside our heads. If it were really the voice of God, I would think it would speak to us a little more consistently."

"Well, sure," I said.

"And self-serving false prophets are everywhere. Just look at all the cult leaders who gained a lot of power, money, and sex by persuading others that they spoke for God. Unless you are a Muslim, you must believe that Muhammad was one of these. Unless you are a Mormon, you must believe that Joseph Smith was also a false prophet. David Koresh, Jim Jones, Sun Myung Moon, and so on. Not to mention that every Mormon break-away sect is led by its own prophet, even though Joseph Smith declared there would only be one true prophet at a time. These religions all provide divine revelations in direct conflict with each other. So, you must necessarily believe that most, if not all, are false prophets."

"What about L. Ron Hubbard? He seems pretty legit," I suggested.

"Well, OK, Hubbard might be for real. I mean, otherwise you would have to be a science fiction writer to come up with a story like Xenu, the galactic dictator who flew billions of his people to earth to blow them up with hydrogen bombs."

"Yarh," I agreed as I swatted at a thetan[i] that attempted to land on me arm.

"So, we know there are false prophets, whether they are psychotic, self-deluding, or self-serving. We only have to prove the last: that there are legitimate prophets who actually hear the voice of God. The problem is that up to now, no one has ever received any so-called 'divine' communication that is distinguishable from the messages delivered by the fakes. In the end, there is no reason to assume a real prophet, the only type that requires a supernatural explanation, even exists."

"But how else would God let us know he's there if he doesn't speak to us through his prophets?" I asked.

"Doesn't a god have unlimited power and all? He could part the clouds and speak to us all at once. He could speak to us in all our minds rather than through a televangelist in an Armani suit and diamond rings. He could make sky writing appear. He could broadcast himself to our TV sets during prime time. He could deliver us a book without scientific mistakes, moral flaws, and doubtful origin, perhaps even one with humorous pirates," Bowtie said, which would later be perceived as rather prophetic.

"The point is, there are lots of ways he could reveal himself and explain his master plan and our purpose in life," Bowtie said. "Instead, we are left trying to interpret vague signs and omens to infer some sort of purpose to be handed to us. We are left with human-written, error-filled scriptures that raise more questions than answers and leave so much to individual interpretation, exactly as if there were no wizard behind the curtain at all."

"But if he just revealed himself, we wouldn't be free to choose to believe in him," I said. "That's what they learned me in Sunday school. We wouldn't have free will."

"FREE WILLIE!" Couscous shouted.

"So, threatening to burn you in eternal Hell for not believing something isn't an infringement of your free will?" Bowtie asked. "Wouldn't it be a better test of moral character and free will if you didn't believe in divine judgement and eternal punishment, but instead acted purely out of concern for your fellow human beings?"

"Aye. Perhaps so," I admitted. "I was never very clear on what the master plan was. I just sort of figured the big guy would explain it all when I got there."

"There? First, we have to look for any evidence of a 'there', before we can even consider that there is a plan to it all."

"But what's the point of living then?" I asked. "I mean, besides the grog and the wenches and all. If life is temporary, why bother with it at all? We come from dust and return to dust."

"Life is, ... ahem, ... is a roast beef sandwich," said Couscous, as he held his up and took a bite.

"What's with the little guy?" I asked, leaning in toward Fettuccini. "What is he? Quinoa?"

"Oh, that's Couscous," Fettuccini said in a whisper. "He's not a grain. He is a very small ball of pasta. Pay him no mind, he's a little retarded."

"Mentally impaired," Seashell corrected him.

Bowtie continued to explain: "Your life, and how you live it is what creates purpose and meaning for you. You begin life with an empty book, and you write it as you go. You are the author, and the author creates the meaning in the story. Most religions try to tell you that you are not in control, but rather God is. Not Pastafarianism, though. Our message is just the opposite: If you don't take an active role in your own life, it will indeed be meaningless. As Couscous said, life is a sandwich. Take a bite out of it."

"Just make it up as I go?" I wondered. "But, again, what is the point? We all die in the end! Why bother with this life?"

Bowtie nodded and said: "Tell me, when you eat a bowl of ice cream, do you sob into it, thinking about how sad it will be when it's all gone?"

"But there's more ice cream in the fridge," I said.

"Let's imagine that the power went out, and it's melting, so you have to eat it all," said Bowtie.

"I can run out and get some more," I replied.

"But with the power out, the store won't have any either," Bowtie explained.

"When the power's back on, the dairy is right down the road, and they can make more," I said.

Bowtie rolled his eyes. A little miffed that his metaphor had a hole in it, methought. "Okay, let's just imagine that you have the last bowl of ice cream in the world, the cows are all dead, sheep too, and the power is out, and what with global warming and all, there is no ice to be found to make any more. So, do you enjoy the last bowl of ice cream or sit there crying about it as it melts?"

I did not feel it appropriate to bring up the possibility of soymilk or some other non-dairy substitute, or the gas-powered generator in my garage. "I suppose I would enjoy the last ice cream on Earth with gusto," I said. "I would make the most of it."

Bowtie smiled. "There, you see? You would close your eyes and savor the flavor. It is all the more precious because that's all there is. Why eat if you'll only get hungry again? Why watch a movie if it comes to an end? Why read a book if it has no sequel? Why take a vacation if you have to go back to work? Why ..."

"I see, I see. It's just hard to accept that this will all come to an end, and I will be no more. A little depressing maybe."

Bowtie nodded. "Life is temporary, which makes it all the more precious. It's like the difference between Coleridge's *The Rime of the Ancient Mariner*, and Robert Frost's *Stopping by Woods on a Snowy Evening*. Frost's poem is much better because it's short and sweet. When you're reading Coleridge, a hundred lines in and you're wondering when does this thing end."

"Aye, I'll agree with you there, mate. I fancy meself more a limerick man"

"You only have so much time here on earth. As Ralph Waldo Emerson said: *Make the most of yourself, for that is all there is of you.*"

"Well then me hearty, tell me more about this cynical thinking," I said.

"Not cynical," Bowtie objected. "*Critical*. The cynic sees only the dark side of human nature. The skeptic distrusts the information, not the person." He paused. "Well, sometimes the person. My point is that critical thinking is a tool. It's a method for learning to think about things, and picking out what's real from what's imaginary, delusional, deception, or just plain crazy. It's a better way of thinking."

"Sounds a bit conceited. I been thinkin' since I was a wee lad," I said. "Are ye saying you're a better thinker than me?"

"Hmmm. Yeah. I suppose I am. But I don't mean that in a conceited way. It's all about the process of *metacognition*: thinking about thinking. Consider this: people who study artistic techniques are better artists. People who study cooking are better cooks. People who study medicine make better doctors."

"Yarh," I nodded, conceding the point.

"So, yes, people who think about thinking, about what influences our thinking, and the ways our brains try to fool us, are probably better thinkers than the average person. And by 'better' I mean that the practiced skeptic is likely to have a more accurate understanding of reality: what is real and what is not."

The young lady seated at the next table suddenly sneezed. Her date had stepped out to the restroom, and she was sitting there alone. She looked at the A-Pastas, who simply stared back at her.

"Well?" she said, after a moment. "Isn't anybody going to bless me?"

The A-Pastas exchanged glances at each other. "None of us are endowed with that magic power," Tortellini said.

"You have a little string of snot hanging from your nose," Penne pointed out.

"The skeptic is seldom popular," Bowtie continued. "We don't get invited to a lot of parties, and our mates get annoyed when we roll our eyes as they read the horoscope column."

"I'm a Pisces, and we don't like know-it-alls," I agreed. "But I don't want to be skeptical. I like to think meself the open-minded sort."

"Oh, but skeptics are not closed-minded! In fact, being skeptical is just the opposite. We consider every aspect of the issue, from all sides of the argument. But we approach extraordinary claims with a healthy degree of doubt," Bowtie said. "People think of skeptics as self-important people who think they know it all. But the ironic thing is that the critical thinker must start from a position of humbleness. The first thing a critical thinker must consider is that he or she could be wrong. We must always be ready to listen to the other person's argument. We must be ready to abandon our position on the issue if there is sound evidence against it. Being stubborn in the face of a good argument leads to faulty thinking."

"Fair enough me hearty," I said.

"Practicing skepticism is merely challenging what is said, and if the evidence supports the claim, you welcome the new information. Close-mindedness is when you reject the evidence that conflicts with what you already believe."

"But ye blokes are always pooh-poohing ancient aliens," I said. "Ye won't even watch the documentaries on the History Channel. They have all kinds of evidence!"

"Yes, I suppose they call it evidence. And the unscrupulous editors take expert opinion out of context and make it look like real scientists support the idea. They are in the entertainment business, not the truth business. As an experienced skeptic, you will find some things that are guaranteed to be wrong, and so you don't waste your time with them. Some topics are the Whack-a-Mole of the pseudoscience world. No matter how many times they are debunked, they keep popping back up. Perpetual motion machines break the laws of physics, and the inventors always seem to abscond with the investor's money. Flat earth theory is mind-numbingly absurd. Cold fusion won't be discovered in someone's garage. Claims of hauntings never turn up testable evidence. We are always left with ghost stories rather than ghost sightings. The closer you examine these things the more they evaporate. Serious paranormal investigators employing scientific rigor find themselves spending a boring night in a so-called haunted house every time. You can only investigate so many of them before you conclude that people follow certain patterns in paranormal claims, be it hoaxing, embellishing, or just plain self-deception."

"Aye, but absence of evidence is not evidence of absence," I said.

"We always start off by giving the benefit of the doubt," Seashell said. "But after more than fifty years of hunting for Bigfoot, what with the advancement in cameras and sensors, there is simply no reasonable way a large, apelike beast could be roaming the forests of North America undetected. All we have to show for it are spurious claims and gorilla suits stuffed with possum guts. When you consider the numerous proven hoaxes and cases of bear fur and footprints, we find trickery and overactive imagination to be more than enough to explain the phenomenon without having to bring in major new assumptions like an absurdly uncommon ability to avoid humans better than any deer or gorilla or snow leopard ever has."

"Yep," Tortellini added, "An island as big as Atlantis, with a kingdom dominating the Mediterranean, leaving behind no trace while every other large society of the day left lots of traces? It just simply never existed. We have a fairly good sonar map of the bottom of the Atlantic Ocean. There is no sunken island that could explain the stories of Plato, the sole source of any story about Atlantis. Plato was clearly using Atlantis as a literary device, which explains why he, of all his contemporaries, was the only one who even mentions it, and with such extensive and descriptive details, all of which he made up. So, when we see yet another claim to have discovered the ruins of Atlantis just off Puerto Rico, we don't hold our breath. We know Atlantis never existed for as certain a fact as we know the Sumerians and the Phoenicians did exist."

"Pictures of ghosts should be getting much sharper with the advancement of technology," Bowtie said. "But they are just as blurry as ever. In these cases, and many others, absence of evidence is indeed evidence of absence."

I did not care to mention that I was a long-time fan of the *Ghost Hunters* TV show. "But isn't Skepticism about doubting everything? Doesn't it just say that we can't really know anything?"

"*Classical skepticism*, as the ancient Greeks taught us, declares that we can never be sure about anything. Take that too far and you will never get any traction trying to understand the world around you. But modern era *Scientific skepticism* tells us we should challenge all prior assumptions, but that as we take careful observation and apply the scientific method, we come closer to an approximate understanding of reality. There are some things we really can know to a high degree of probability and accuracy. But that knowledge always comes with the caveat that if better evidence comes along which changes our understanding, we must be ready to adapt."

"Yarh. So, critical thinking be the same thing as skepticism?" I asked.

"They both go hand in hand. *Skepticism* is the opposite of credulity and gullibility. *Critical thinking* is more about the metacognition we use to try to be as objective as possible and applying the scientific process where needed: hypothesize, test, evaluate, repeat. *Skepticism* is the guard we put up, whereas *critical thinking* is the means of determining what ideas get past the guard and into our heads."

"Blimey, mate. Ye make a simple thing like thinking into something hard," I said. "I knows what I know."

"We all use shortcut reasoning. It is natural and necessary for us to use simple heuristics, what we call *rules of thumb*, to get by day-to-day. We all do it, even the practiced skeptic, because we don't have the time or patience to examine everything that we encounter," said Bowtie. "Critical thinking on the other hand is unnatural. Our natural reasoning is fundamentally biased. We fool ourselves in many ways. We use *motivated reasoning* to ensure our conclusions fit our pre-conceived notions."

And Linguine added: "We also tend to think tribally. We go with the crowd in order to keep peace. We hold our most ingrained beliefs not because they are logically true, but because we were born into them and they form a part of who we are. If we break from the tribe's belief, we break from the tribe and our identity."

Bowtie continued: "It's not easy to be a critical thinker. It must be learned, honed, applied, and practiced like any discipline. Just being aware of biases and self-deceiving thought patterns does not make you immune to the problem of warping reality to fit your belief. No one ever completely avoids irrational thinking. But if we work at it, separating our emotional response and mental bias from objective facts, we begin to think more rationally."

"Otherwise, you're a NINCOMPOOP!" said Couscous.

"Shiver me timbers," I exclaimed. "I don't want to be a nincompoop. Where do we start?"

"The first step is to admit you are a nincompoop," said Bowtie. "The second step is to identify the stumbling blocks to rational thought."

"Like what?" I asked.

"When you feel that surge of passion about a topic, you should raise a red flag. You are going to have a hard time thinking critically about anything that you have an emotional stake in. Think of anything that gets you riled up. Politics? Abortion? Global warming? Kirk or Picard?

"Don't get me started! But are ye sayin' I can't think straight?"

"Sometimes our thinking gets commandeered. Most of the time we are not really looking for the truth. Instead we are looking for confirmation of what we already believe. I figure you for the Kirk type, but you have to admit Picard was clearly smarter."

Me hand instinctively reached for me sword.

"We readily accept claims which support our ideas and are quick to reject those which refute them. We accept weak logic when it suits us. Our biases and preconceived notions conspire to warp our reasoning skills to ensure that we reach the conclusion that we want. But if we really want to understand, we need to accept reality, warts and all."

"Gorn would have kicked Picard's ass," I said. "But tell me more."

"It would be best if I showed you. You wouldn't happen to have a brain around, would you?"

I looked around and spied young Bob Woodcock, the cabin boy from my ship, sitting in the corner, texting on his phone. "Young master Robert," I called. "Come join us, me lad." He looked up timidly, not sure if he was the Robert I was referring to, as we had several Roberts on the crew. But at the prospect of a free drink, he shyly came over to our table. "Fellas, meet Bob Woodcock, our cabin boy."

"He'll do," Bowtie said. "Have a seat my good man."

"SKNORK ..."

Bowtie stood up behind the boy and proceeded to poke around the back of his head. Woodcock looked a wee bit surprised, wondering why a complete stranger might be feeling up his skull, I'm sure. "There is usually a latch back here somewhere," Bowtie explained. "Ah, there it is."

"SHKEEE SHKEE SHKEE ..."

Bowtie pressed inward and the lid of the boy's skull popped open. Woodcock's eyes rolled up and went shut as he passed out.

"SNORT ..."

"What is it, Couscous?" Bowtie said, getting a little annoyed.

"*WOODCOCK!* Kheee kheee..."

"Oh, grow up," Seashell said. Couscous went back to gnawing on his roast beef sandwich.

"Have a look here," Bowtie said to me, lifting the hairy crown off and setting it aside to reveal what was inside the boy's head. The young lady at the next table abruptly stopped her story about her roommate.

"Avast," I exclaimed, peering into the boy's braincase, "What be that thick goop?"

"This is the sludge of prior beliefs. It slows down the efficient processing of information. This is part of the Bayesian thought process."

"Bayesian? You'll have to explain that one, matey. I was a liberal arts major."

"The Bayesian process is a logical method of calculating the probability that a hypothesis is true based on new information compared to previous information. There is a formal mathematical approach, and usually takes the new information as an observed, objective measurement, which is added to the calculation as either supporting or opposing evidence. But I am informally referring to the general principle in a backwards way. Here I reverse the logic: the solidness of our pre-conceived ideas, and the depth of our stake in the issue, determines our resistance to the new information based on whether the new information agrees or disagrees."

"So, if we already understand something well enough and have seen a lot of evidence," Seashell added, "and someone tells you something that confirms what you believed before, it is more easily accepted as true. But when a claim runs counter to a well-established concept, it should be more thoroughly challenged."

"Exactly," said Bowtie. "For example, having read a thick stack of books and science journal articles on evolution and natural history, when I encounter a news item by young-earth creationists that they have found footprints of humans walking with dinosaurs, my first reaction is to reject the claim, until they can provide independent scientific review to confirm it."

"Yarh, I get it. Ye doubt what doesn't fit the way ye understand things," I said.

"Yup. When your first mate blames the missing rum on a pack of ravaging mermaids, and you know full well mermaids are more the vodka martini types, you begin to doubt his story and smell his breath."

"Aye. Mermaid breath smells like fish," I said. "The first mate's smells like mermaid."

"And the stranger the claim, the more important it is that we start from a position of doubt. As I always say, *extraordinary claims require extraordinary evidence.*"

"Can I quote ye on that?"

"Quote Carl Sagan, who was probably quoting others before him. It has been the skeptic's mantra for a long time. But we also need to be wary of the other side of the coin. We resist new information that disagrees with what we have always believed. We close our minds to counter-ideas. If we were raised to believe something, like a religious tenet or racial prejudice, it is hard for us to cut through the brain-sludge and accept new ideas that run counter to it."

"And when we don't want to change our minds, we have a whole toolkit of ways to avoid the evidence, like *confirmation bias*, *cherry picking*, and *motivated reasoning*," Seashell added.

"Wait, go back to that *confirmation bias*," I said.

"When we see or hear something that confirms what we already believe, we notice and accept it," Seashell explained. "When it does not confirm our beliefs, we tend to ignore it."

Then the fat one, Ravioli, jumped in to add: "If you believe in clairvoyance, you notice the psychic's occasional lucky hits, but don't keep track of the many misses. And I'm stuffed, not fat."

"I didn't say anything," I said. Shiver me timbers! It was like he was reading my mind.

Ravioli continued: "Most people don't understand the mathematical probability of intuitive, non-psychic guesses used in *cold reading*."

"What's this *cold reading*?" I asked.

"Cold reading is a technique where the 'psychic' makes a few highly probable guesses, or a lot of less probable guesses, and tracks your reactions, probing forward as you confirm hits and pass on misses. For example, you work with someone with a name that begins with an 'R', or a 'B'," he said.

"Robert?"

"Robert. That's it."

"The cockswain or the first mate?" I asked.

"Cockswain?"

"Avast! How did you know?" I asked.

"I just knew," said Ravioli. "The point is, you readily accept things that confirm what you believe, and don't notice the rest, and most of the information is what you provided, not the so-called psychic."

"The really good psychics use *hot reading*," said Seashell, "Where you use internet research, surveys, and accomplices planted in the audience to pick up clues about personal information that you would think nobody could have known."

"There is also the sunken-cost bias," Bowtie added. "You paid two shillings for your fortune, so you want to feel you got your money's worth and not just admit that it was wasted. And when you retell the tale, you will want your listener to believe it as much as you do, so you're motivated to embellish the details to make it sound more amazing and undeniable than it really was. If you tell these artificial details often enough, they become embedded in your memory as though that was how it really happened."

"Brain sludge. Hmm," I said, looking down into the boy's skull again. "It's a bit lumpy, like me Aunt Maria's beef gravy."

"The lumps are emotional investments, your stake in the belief. The more emotionally attached you are to a prior belief, the more it clumps up and hardens, and the harder it is to penetrate with reason."

Bowtie plunged his hand into the goop and pulled out a pair of devices with little dials and displays on them, connected to each other by a flexible copper tube.

"I'll be hornswoggled! What be that contraption?"

"This is your *Cognitive Empathy Processor*, or CEP," he said, holding up the first device which had an array of wires running into the front. "*Cognitive Empathy* means thinking about what someone else is thinking. You see these connections running from the eyes and ears into it? It takes in the words and non-verbal cues of other people, and helps you figure out what is going on in the minds of others. We call that *theory of mind*. When your *theory of mind* is broken, you have Autism."

"Aye," I said. "You mentioned theory of mind back in the first gospel."

"I did? Well, that was written after my death, so I wouldn't know. I hope I'm not being redundant. Anyway, when this isn't working, other people are just things to you."

"But on the other hand," added Seashell, "If your CEP is cranked up too high, you start putting thoughts and feelings into things that aren't even alive. We see this in the hyper-religious. This is sometimes called *hyperactive agency detection*."

"But it's a completely natural tendency," Bowtie explained. "Most people attribute some degree of agency to things like dolls or stuffed animals, so much so that we feel sympathy for them. It's irresistible. In fact, these things are purposely designed to evoke our empathy. That's why we latch onto them as children and take them with us wherever we go. We feel a little sad for that lonely teddy bear when we grow older and stop playing with it. But it's not alive. It has no feelings. Even the critical thinker can't shut it off, but he or she should at least be aware of the effect."

I nearly teared up, thinking about me Pookey upstairs in the bottom of me footlocker.

Bowtie flipped the devices around to show the other gadget connected to the Cognitive Empathy Processor. "This is the *Affective Empathy Modulator*, or AEM. If the Cognitive Empathy Processor is the input device, the AEM is the output. The AEM takes input from the CEP and lets you respond with appropriate emotion. This device is what makes your brain act with concern when you see others upset or makes you happy when you see others are happy. When you hurt someone's feelings and realize you need to apologize, this is the thing that pushes you to do so. Some people have this thing set too low, and they come off as a bit cold and emotionless, like an Ayn Rand devotee."

Ravioli tapped the device and said: "In the sociopath, this is turned off altogether. They don't feel any real compassion, and their emotional range is usually restricted to their own ego, such as envy and rage. The sociopath can put on a show, though. Their CEP is usually working just fine. They can understand what is going on in your mind and can use it against you. They know just how to poke your buttons by pretending to have the emotions that the Affective Empathy Modulator should be making them feel for real. Instead of an AEM, the sociopath has an *Affective Empathy Simulator*. They use their simulator to project a feigned emotion to fool your theory of mind, to make you imagine that they are concerned for you or are only acting out of the goodness of their heart. That is how they get you where they want you *[Denworth, 2017]*."

"THE BASTARDS!" yelled Couscous.

"Does he always talk in ALLCAPS?" I asked.

"Mostly. But that brings us around to the next thing I want to show you." Bowtie followed a coaxial cable back into the goop and pulled out a third device, one that looked like a small espresso machine with a pressure dial on it. "This is your *Bastardostat*. It sets your baseline level of meanness. The sociopath is on the high end of the spectrum, but some people are just plain mean without trying to take advantage of you the way the sociopath does. This is the source of *Schadenfreude*, the pleasure some of us derive from the misery of others."

"So, these things affect your empathy and meanness. I savvy. But how do they relate to critical thinking?" I asked.

"These three devices are part of your moral constitution. They affect your values, which in turn affect your reasoning."

Bowtie pulled them a little further out of the skull and held them up. "As far as critical thinking goes, remember that when the Cognitive Empathy Processor is cranked too high, you may be attributing agency, or intention, to things that are not capable of having it. You might be convinced your pet lizard has undying love for you, or you might be paranoid and think that everyone is out to get you. However, in the cases of the autistic, in which the CEP is not working, and the sociopath, who feels no empathy, these people sometimes see things more clearly than the rest of us precisely because their emotions do not cloud their reasoning as much."

"So, are ye saying we should think like sociopaths and autistics?" I asked.

"Well, sort of. I'm not saying you should suppress your empathy and emotions. This would be a horrible place if we all thought like sociopaths. The world needs compassion. But you should be aware of your emotional biases and their effect on your reasoning. You should understand how you might be predisposed against evidence or logic that runs counter to your emotional stake in the matter."

Bowtie draped the wires over the side of Bob's open skull and set the three devices on the table.

"We all have a set of values, and values affect your emotional response to things, rather than your understanding of things. But your emotional response can affect your reasoning. You might reject something as a possibility simply because it runs so counter to your values. A good example is a study showing how carefully managed trophy hunting in Africa might actually be helping conservation efforts."
[Alexander, Mathieson & Romanach, 2006]

"Yahrr, killin' innocent animals for the fun of it," I shook me head. "How can that be good?"

"I find it kind of offensive too, but we have to put aside our knee-jerk reaction and look at the data."

Bowtie wiped the sludge from his hands with a bar towel, which drew a scowl from the barkeep.

"I have a few more components to show you which can cause you to warp reality to fit what you want to believe." He plucked out another device, this one with a shiny gold finish underneath the blood and brain sludge and held it up. "The *Greedometer* determines just how selfish you are. Bob's reading is a little low for a pirate. When you stand to gain a lot from one conclusion over another, your reasoning is likely to be motivated, and even more so when you are selfish. Privateers figure it's not really stealing when they raid enemy merchant vessels in the name of the king. It's just part of the war effort, a part that happens to make them rich."

The angel-hairy one, Capellini, explained: "For example, if you run a coal mine, you stand to lose your livelihood if the government determines that fossil-fuel driven global warming is a problem and enacts laws to encourage renewable energy. So, you will heavily weight any argument against global warming."

And Ravioli said: "If you sell sugary drinks, but medical evidence exposes its role in diabetes, you might be quick to dismiss the study. Your company might even pay people to put out misinformation like the cigarette companies did when scientists determined tobacco causes cancer."

Bowtie added: "There is a popular idea in Oklahoma that the increase in earthquakes in that area is being caused by windmills, and not the oil shale fracking that is making so many people rich."

Bowtie handed the Greedometer to Tortellini, who fiddled with it a bit before setting it aside on the table. "Greed and self-interest are necessary ingredients in the big picture of human psychology, of course. The scientific term for a species that bears zero self-interest is '*extinct*'. But we often dismiss facts that work against our personal interest."

Fig. #1 Forkscrew removed from the head of Robert Woodcock

Bowtie reached in along the right temple of Bob's braincase, and located an ugly device with twisted, pointy shards of metal splayed in all directions. It came off with a strong tug after a bit of difficulty, Bowtie nearly cutting his fingers in the process. "This is the *forkscrew*," Bowtie said, wiping a bit of brain gunk off his chin with his sleeve. "This is the thing that makes your brain hurt to admit you were wrong. It is the *forkscrew* that causes us to double down and deny obvious evidence to the contrary. We all have one of these, but if you really work at it, you can reduce the pain and even learn to appreciate the ability to change your mind for the better."

Tortellini took this too and set it beside the other pieces.

"We might leave that out when we put him back together," Bowtie murmured to himself as he poked around inside Bob's cranium. "There should be somewhere around here ..." He abruptly turned and lifted the hairy crown off the table and flipped it over. "Ah, here it is," he said as he pulled out a valve which had been attached to the inside top. "This is the *Apathy Regulator*. In fact, Bob's is a model APR-1227, which if I remember correctly was recalled a few years back. He needs to go in for an upgrade. It's a very important device. If you didn't have this, you would be uncontrollably concerned about everything. You'd drive yourself mad. Bob's is set a little too low, though. He's a caring sort. I'll just turn it up a bit. Not too high. The scientific term for a species with too much apathy is ..."

"I know, I know. *Extinct*," I said.

"Correctamundo." Bowtie laid the apathy regulator on the table. Tortellini picked it up and turned the adjusting lever back and forth a few times. "Stop playing with that," Bowtie warned.

Bowtie stared intently into the boy's open head, trying to track something moving inside. He hovered just above the dark liquid for a moment, and then suddenly plunged both hands in and pulled out a squirming, wriggling black thing that looked like a bat without wings. "This is *Fear*," Bowtie held it up triumphantly. "Fear has an amazingly powerful influence on our thought processes. Fear of being eaten prompts us to assume that the rustle in the bushes is a tiger. Fear of snakes and spiders causes us to kill them without hesitation, regardless of the important roles these critters have in the ecosystem."

Taking it from Bowtie, Tortellini grabbed a bar towel and wrapped the Fear in it. "And fear of Hell makes people afraid to not believe their hell-fire preachers," Tortellini said. He set it on the table, but it kept squirming under the towel, wiggling its way to the edge. Tortellini picked up a heavy ashtray and slammed it down on top of the Fear, making it go still.

"Careful, Tortellini," Bowtie scolded. "Fear is a necessary brain component. If you damage that, the poor boy will be swinging from the yardarms like a monkey."

Bowtie then reached deep into the skull, sinking his arm in nearly to the elbow, and came up with the end of a rusty chain. He slowly pulled out about three feet of chain, at the end of which was attached a small wooden chest with leather straps and a keyhole. "Here we have it! This is an important part." He set it proudly on the table with a heavy thud as slimy goop dripped down its sides. "This is the boy's *Existential Angst*."

The young lady at the next table stood up and announced to her date that it was time to go.

"Are ye sure ye should be messing with that?" I asked.

"Shall we take a look inside?"

"I'd prefer ye did not," I said.

"You might ask yourself why most people in all cultures around the world believe in some variation of an afterlife or perpetual rebirth, given that there is no scientific evidence for it. The answer is *Existential Angst*. They can't handle our inevitable fate of non-existence. Most people will never open this chest. They keep it safely locked up by clinging to their insistence on an afterlife, as though their sheer stubbornness can make it go away. Death has always been nipping at the heels of every being that has ever lived, and it invariably wins. Survival instinct is the most stress-inducing force within us all. Do you know what they call …"

"*Extinct*," I said curtly.

He thumped the little black chest with his hand and continued: "As humankind gradually evolved intelligence and self-awareness, we have had to come to terms with the fact that everyone dies. But most of us choose to avoid the reality of death."

"Religion lets us pretend we don't die," Seashell said. "That's why we cling to it so dearly."

Bowtie nodded. "It all began when a parent, intending to soothe the fears of her child, first told him a story of a wonderful place you go to when you die. Heaven was born, and ever since then we have used religion to avoid what is locked away inside this chest, our *Existential Angst*. It lies there, in the pit of our stomach, and the lock is only as strong as our belief in an afterlife. As we practice critical thinking, even this sacred cow must be addressed."

"Yarh, I could use a spot of rum about now."

"This is, I think, our primary motivator for pretending in religion. We fear death, our own and our loved ones', so we try to pretend there is an afterlife. Fear of random danger makes us pretend angels are watching out for us. Fear of injustice for the wronged makes us pretend there is a righteous judgement awaiting the evil among us, especially those we cannot bring to justice ourselves. We fear a meaningless life, so we imagine there is a divine meaning in our existence, that we are not here by chance. And yet, in spite of what we tell ourselves to make death disappear, *Existential Angst* is always there, gnawing at our souls. Dig deep down, open the chest and let the light in. Confront it!"

"That thar be some pretty heavy shit coming from an anthropomorphic piece of pasta," I said. "Why don't ye just let people believe in an afterlife if they can't handle reality? I figure, if it makes them feel better, why not?"

"The reason so many people can't handle reality is because they have never been exposed to it. I propose that the most mentally healthy approach is to confront this reality early and openly, rather than letting it fester in a pool of doubt in the back of our minds, waiting for a crisis of faith before it rears its ugly head. We need to recognize that life is temporary, but just as precious, or even more so because it is temporary. We need to acknowledge that we were non-existent for billions of years, and we will once again be non-existent for countless billions more. In the grand scheme of eternity our lives are but a blink of the eye. But we don't live at that scale. We live within the context of our own beginning and end, and so we should make every moment count. We should enjoy this life for what it is rather than live in a fantasy about a better world to come."

"Aye," I said. "But couldn't ye soften the blow a bit? It be pretty harsh just to tell people they be worm food."

"It's only your body that becomes worm food. The part of you that makes you special, your sentience, will never experience death itself, because death is the absence of sentience."

We were getting near the bottom of the brain. I spied a sparkly crystal thingamabob, about the size of my thumb, but diamond shaped. "And what be that?" I said, pointing at it.

"Glad you asked. That is an *Ignorance Amazulator*." Bowtie pulled the crystal out and held it up to the light. "There, do you see it?" he whispered.

"See what?"

"The unicorn. There is a tiny little unicorn inside it."

I stared into the crystal, and there, to my flabbergasted amazement, was a little rainbow-colored unicorn with a tiny little horn on his head. "What does it do?" I asked.

"Think of something really complex, like how consciousness arises from the physical brain, or how cellular biology works. Mind boggling, isn't it? But your brain can't comprehend the complexity. To ease the uncomfortable feeling of not understanding, this little device comes to the rescue."

"It must be magic. I can't imagine how that would work!" I said.

"Exactly!" explained Bowtie. "The tiny little unicorn whispers in your ear that it is magic. If you can't understand it, it must be of supernatural origin. This little unicorn in the crystal is the source of the whole branch of pretend science we call *Intelligent Design*. '*I can't understand something so therefore: magic.*' *Intelligent Design* is based on the idea that some biological structures are so interdependent on their constituent parts that they could not have developed from something simpler. Any simpler version would be useless and so would not have evolved, and therefore must have been created by an intelligent designer. This is the principle of *irreducible complexity*."

"Sounds reasonable to me," I said.

"But when scientists closely examine these mind-bogglingly complex things, they find that there are indeed simpler precursors to be found. Every example of so-called irreducible complexity that ID proponents have come up with has been thoroughly refuted, albeit in lengthy scientific papers which are usually either beyond the comprehension or outside the cognitive bias of the average ID adherent. Most supporters of ID rarely take the time to even read the rebuttals, mostly because they don't care, since it is the layman out there that they are trying to convince with their arguments, not the serious scientist. They are not trying to win the legitimate argument. They are only interested in convincing enough people of their ideas to get equal time with real science in the classroom. The really amazing thing is that no matter how much evidence-based scientific literature or well-thought-out evolutionary theory you present to refute the claims of *Intelligent Design*, such as papers on the intermediate evolutionary structures of bacterial flagellum, they keep returning with the same arguments, because they know that you, too, have a tiny little unicorn inside your head."

Bowtie examined the crystal, tapping it to make the unicorn look up. "It helps the Intelligent Design cause that there is a strong desire among most people to believe in it. They are motivated to believe by emotional investments, cultural customs, fear of erosion of their religion, and even that forkscrew we just looked at. They fear the implication that maybe the *good book* was just plain wrong. If the Genesis creation story is myth, what parts of the Bible can be trusted?"

"Yarh. I was fine with the talking snake, but the talking donkey goes a bit too far," I said.

"If they were trying to introduce divine magic as a counter-theory to aerodynamics in the science curriculum, nobody would ever give them the time of day." He held the crystal out for Tortellini to set aside. "But *Intelligent Design* is seriously proposed for inclusion in our children's formal education system every few years, and those in favor of keeping education legitimate have to fight them again and again."

Tortellini took the Ignorance Amazulator and carefully placed it on the table. No sooner had he put the thing down than Couscous jumped up, grabbed the ashtray and smashed the crystal, yelling: "YOU ARE FREE, LITTLE UNICORN!" The tiny unicorn climbed out of the broken crystal, and ran and leaped off the table, disappearing in an arc of sparkling rainbow light.

"Couscous!" yelled Seashell.

"It's okay," said Bowtie. "Mr. Woodcock will be better off without it."

"WOODCOCK!" squealed Couscous.

"Couscous, what did I teach you about making fun of people's names?"

"Don't," said Couscous.

"Now, where was I?" Bowtie turned back to young master Woodcock and began to feel around in the liquid, seized something that seemed to be trying to evade his hand, and announced: "Everybody cover your ears. This might be loud." He pulled up something that looked like a blood-soaked fortune cookie. On meeting the air, it began to screech, a shrill, clawing tone that pierced the eardrums. He quickly set it on the floor and stomped with his boot as hard as he could. "Ah, Bob! I don't know how you managed with that in your head."

"What was it?" I asked.

"That was *cognitive dissonance*. It looks like young Woodcock here subscribed to the story of Adam and Eve but had recently been to the natural history museum and wandered through the collection of hominin skulls. That must have been painful, trying to keep both concepts in his head at once. Seems he was trying to imagine Adam and Eve looking like apes, then had to reconcile with God creating man in his own chimp-like image. It's sort of like having both a cat and a girlfriend with an allergy. Eventually one of them has to go."

"KEEP THE CAT!" Couscous yelled.

I picked the crushed cognitive dissonance up from the floor to examine it closer. "I never knew there were such contraptions in the human head."

"Oh, there's more. Take this *Confabulator*." Bowtie said, pulling out a bulbous blue organ. "Listen to it!"

A steady drone of words flowed from the Confabulator: "… *cat has an allergy and that's why the girlfriend was sneezing, because the apes lived in the Garden of Eden with the tiny unicorn …*" It all seemed to flow from one thought to the next yet making no sense at all.

"This provides our narrative. We typically don't notice it, because it normally provides a fairly reasonable story. We only notice it's effects when it gets a bit crazy, most commonly as the illogical events of our dreams. But dreams usually don't transfer into our long-term memory, and most are strange enough that we recognize them as dreams, so we seldom confuse them with waking memories."

"Yarh. I had a dream I was eating a giant marshmallow," I started to say.

"And your pillow was gone in the morning," Bowtie said. "We also see the Confabulator at work when experiencing sleep deprivation, sensory deprivation, extreme stress, drugs, or brain damage. These can sometimes let the Confabulator run unchecked. It might be trying to make sense of inexplicable behavior after a stroke, or why we did something embarrassing or bizarre. In these cases, impairment prevents our sorting out reality from the confabulation. Our brains can't tell the difference. *[Sternberg, 2015]*"

"That explains the crazy shit that comes out of Robert the coxswain's mouth after a pint of rum," I said.

Bowtie listened to the Confabulator some more. "He's dreaming. Sometimes, when you are just waking up, your brain is still receiving nonsense input from your brainstem, and the Confabulator does it's best to turn it into a story for you. Your remembered experience might come in the shape of a ghost, or a vision. All memories, whether based on sensory input from the real world or internal activity within the brain are stored and recalled the same. Paradoxically, sometimes the product of the Confabulator seems more real to you than reality itself."

"Ye be tellin' me that memory is not the tape recorder I always thought it was?"

"The more you understand how memories work, the more you begin to distrust your own brain. This is one place where healthy skepticism of your own recollections actually makes you fare worse in an argument. The skeptic is always second-guessing himself."

"Or herself," said Penne.

"Thanks, Penne. I am trying to keep things respectfully gender neutral." Bowtie looked a little irritated. He set the Confabulator on the table, then reached in and pulled out a black, tube-like thing about five inches long. As he wiped it off, he explained: "And here is something related to the Confabulator. It's a *pattern recognition* flashlight. You shine it on stuff and you see things that aren't there!"

The one called Linguine jumped up and said: "Oooh, let me do it! I love that thing!" He took the flashlight, turned it on, and pointed it at the wood grain on the wall. "I see an old man with a beard!" he said. And indeed, there was something in the wood that looked like a bearded old man.

"Let me set it to *Cat*!" said Linguine, rotating a knob on the device. He pointed it at a dog curled up in the corner, and in the yellowish beam of light, it appeared to have cat ears and a tabby coat. This annoyed the dog to no end. If you looked hard enough at it, you could see the dog, but any quick glance would turn it instantly into a cat. In fact, there appeared to be cats all around the room as Linguine swung the flashlight around.

"You see, the optical nerve running from the eye to the brain does not have high enough throughput to transmit the whole picture that appears in your head. The brain keeps reference images. It knows what a cat looks like, so if enough of an image comes through to make it cat-like, the brain will fill in the details of *'catness'* until the rest of the image arrives. *[Dennett, 1991; Sternberg, 2015]* The shortcoming in this process is that we are primed to see a lot of one thing, that which is the easiest pattern to match. Our brain may see something that is just not there, simply because we were expecting to see it. And where the input is fairly random, such as wood grain, tile patterns, or a water stain on concrete, if enough of the image matches something familiar, the brain fills in the rest, resulting in a phenomenon called pareidolia. But remember, this thing is inside your head, so the same thing happens with other inputs. You might hear human voices in a gurgling drain or a buzzing fan. And it can affect whole thought processes. This is how you develop conspiracy theories from news articles and rumors as you piece things together into an interrelated pattern that may or may not be real. When this thing is hyperactive, you might be diagnosed as schizophrenic."

"I wish it were daytime," said Linguine, "Because if we were to step outside and look at the clouds, this thing would go crazy." He handed the pattern recognition flashlight to Tortellini.

Tortellini turned the knob to a new setting and called out: "Anybody have a piece of toast?" The bartender had some he was saving for salad croutons on the Sunday buffet, and offered it. Linguine shined the flashlight on it, and there, for all to see, was *Our Lord and Savior Jesus Christ* ™.

"That is so cool!" Tortellini exclaimed.

Couscous jumped up and tried to grab the flashlight from Tortellini, but it fell on the floor and the light went off. The lens popped out and rolled into a heating grate.

"You idiot!" yelled Linguine. "Look what you've done. You broke it."

Bowtie sighed. "That flashlight is really important! If it's not working, the boy won't recognize anything! Bears, insurance salesmen, Brazilian prostitutes. He'll fall prey to whatever comes along. Vermicelli! Fettuccini! See if you can open that grate and find it."

Linguine picked up the flashlight and unscrewed the end, trying to reseat the battery as the others moved tables to one side and began to pry up the floor grate with a bottle opener.

"That's about it. We probably ought to start putting everything back like we found it," Bowtie said, looking at the Confabulator, rotating it until it looked like it might fit where he had pulled it out from. "You know, I probably should have washed my hands before I started digging in here," Bowtie thought aloud to himself.

"Well, thank ye for the brain lesson," I said. "I wouldn't have pegged ye as a neurologist when ye walked in here."

"Oh, I am not a neurologist. I am a holy man. Well, holy pasta, anyway."

"But how do ye know all this?" I inquired.

"Years of reading *Scientific American* and listening to podcasts."

"And that makes ye qualified to open a man's brain and pull things out?" I asked.

Bowtie stared at me a moment, then said: "Have I told you I am the son of the Flying Spaghetti Monster?"

"Yes," I said. "That was how this whole conversation started."

"Well, did you know that you have a pasta-shaped hole in your heart?"

"My doctor called it *angina*," I said.

"Found it!" yelled Vermicelli, holding up the flashlight lens.

"Well, tell me more about this Flying Spaghetti Monster dad of yours," I said.

"In Heaven there are beer volcanos ..." Bowtie began, and the conversation lasted deep into the night.

A few days later, the A-Pastas signed on to me crew as mates and after a few marauding adventures along the Barbary Coast, we landed in New Jersey. To make a long story short and not be redundant like some holy scriptures, when we got there, a bunch of mad people boiled Bowtie and ate him. He remained unrisen, and we never saw the likes of him again after that, just as the prophecy said.

And that's me story. By the way, if they ever make this into a movie, please do not use Johnny Depp for my role. I picture meself more the Orlando Bloom type.

The Gospel of Greenbeard

This is the gospel of Greenbeard, or rather a gospel with Greenbeard in it, since Greenbeard didn't actually write this, what with him being dead and all. This account is related by the collective memory of Capellini, Ravioli, and Tortellini over a case of beer and a Grand Theft Auto tournament, with corrections by Seashell when she reviewed it the next day, having found the manuscript while cleaning up Cheetos which were everywhere, the filthy pigs. In that way, it's kind of like the Gospel of John, which was written long after the disciple John would have been dead, except that this gospel was actually written by eyewitnesses to the events.

As Bowtie and his A-Pastas were sailing along the Barbary Coast, they neared an island and saw a strange man on the beach, a pirate by his attire, sporting a green beard, and jumping from rock to rock. He would occasionally yell something or other, but he was not calling to Bowtie or the ship. He seemed to be yelling into the air, taking a few steps, jumping back, and starting off in a different direction. At one point, the weird fellow stopped, tilted his head back, and balanced several pebbles on his forehead for no apparent reason.

"What an odd little man," Tortellini said as he stood beside Bowtie at the ship's railing.

"WEIRDO!" yelled Couscous.

"Be nice, Couscous," Bowtie admonished. He then called to the captain and asked to make landfall to see if the man needed assistance. Soon a dinghy was dispatched with Bowtie, Tortellini, Capellini, Seashell, and two sailors at the oars. Wading ashore, Bowtie called out to the man, who suddenly looked up, almost shocked to find he was not alone, which was peculiar as he could not have missed a three-masted schooner weighing anchor 300 feet away.

"Avast! Who be ye?" the green-bearded pirate called.

"I am Bowtie, son of the Flying-" Bowtie replied, but was abruptly cut off.

"SCRAMBLED RACOON BALLS!" the pirate yelled.

"WTF?" Tortellini wondered, eyebrows raised. "What madness has taken this man?"

"Bet you didn't see that coming," the pirate added.

"Indeed, I didn't," said Bowtie. "What-"

"HARPSICHORD IN THE HOLE!" the green-bearded man yelled again.

"Ah, ..." Bowtie began, wondering if further conversation might be pointless. "What may I ask is your name, sir?"

"Greenbeard," the man replied. "Greenbeard the Pirate, at your service. PICKLED POPSICLES!"

"Why do you keep doing that?" Tortellini asked.

"Tortellini," Bowtie said turning toward him, "Please be polite. Don't you see, the man obviously has Tourette Syndrome. He has no control over it."

"Shiver me timbers, no, not at all," Greenbeard clarified. "That's just the point! I am in complete control of everything I say. LOBSTER PUDDING!"

"I see," Bowtie said. "So then can you explain why you keep yelling out absurd, irrelevant phrases?"

"Free will!" Greenbeard said. "I am trying to prove that I have free will. I can say and do whatever I choose. CHOCOLATE BUNGALOWS! You see? I am not an automaton. No robot here."

"Ah. That explains it. You've read Sam Harris's *Free Will*," said Bowtie, referring to the popular book, which in contradiction to the title, is all about how we don't have any.

"NEVER! I did not, and a lubber like you can't deduce that from me actions." Greenbeard stood quietly for a moment, then looked down dejectedly. "Aye, I read it. And ever since, I've been on this deity-forsaken island, trying to prove to the world that I can do whatever I want, with free will. Alas, all for naught. I am a biological robot, a victim of my clockwork brain." He sighed deeply.

"Who is a victim of your brain?" Bowtie asked.

"Me. I am a victim of the deterministic choices my brain makes. Science proves it."

"But who is the victim?"

"*Me*! Are ye hard of hearing, matey?" Greenbeard posed on one leg, left foot tucked behind his right knee, and made moose antlers with his cupped hands. "If I have no free will, and Sam Harris says I don't, I would be a victim of myself, don't you see?"

"But that necessarily implies two distinct things: you and your brain. When you self-reference with the relative pronoun, *me*, what are you referring to if not to the consciousness generated by the functions of your brain? You are your brain. There is no one else inside your skull to be a victim. It's all you. The rest of your body is just a machine your brain uses to get around. The idea that someone can be a victim of their own brain would seem to imply a notion of dualism: a supernatural soul as the victim of a material body." *[Alcock, 2018, Chapter 10, and Dennett, 1991. Also google Mind-body Dualism]*[ii]

Greenbeard furrowed his brow as he pondered this. "If I were the same, atom for atom, as a serial killer or a rapist, I would make the same choices, according to Sam. How could I be held accountable for my actions if I did what my serial killer brain told me to do?"

Bowtie shook his head. "Oh, I don't doubt that you would be a serial killer if, atom for atom, you were a serial killer. But then you wouldn't be the pirate Greenbeard, and the serial killer does what serial killers do because he or she chooses to do it. Sam Harris takes his description of *free will* directly from the religious authorities, as requiring some sort of immaterial origin. If *free will* is the ability to make choices independent of a physical process inside our brain, we set a standard that necessarily renders it impossible without a supernatural explanation. This definition leaves two possibilities: that thinking is either physical, and therefore *deterministic*, or supernaturally independent of the physical state of our brain, and therefore *free will*. But it all comes down to how we define free will, and I don't find this definition very useful." [iii]

"What else could it be?" Greenbeard asked. "If thinking is all a mechanical process, then it must be deterministic. Surely the thought process is just the machinery in our head, dependent upon our neurons and how they are wired together. How can I control that? I am a meat robot."

"Our brains function in a way that is neither entirely independent nor entirely deterministically against our will. We have *urges*, the desire to do a thing, and we have *will*, the self-control to fight our urges when they conflict with our values. When they conflict, people to varying degrees, depending upon their degree of thoughtfulness and self-control, usually act according to their will, not their urges."

"Aye, like when me balls itch in public," said Greenbeard.

"Ah, yes, I suppose," said Bowtie, wondering if that was a supporting point or a counter example. "We all have values, moral or non-moral, some learned and some innate. Add to that various bits of information concerning the thing we are mulling over, and we make decisions based upon what seems reasonable to us. We work out logic because words and thoughts have meaning and consequences beyond a positive or negative synaptic connection, and this meaning is processed through our value system. And values can be cultivated. Your values reflect your culture, not your genetics. They are taught to you, often in church and schools, but also in the family setting. They are a reflection of when and where you grew up. But we are not slaves to them. They can and do change as we mature and self-reflect. Reading a book or news article can change them."

"Well, that might be so for some," Greenbeard said. "My values might be a bit impaired, having grown up in Milwaukie."

"I agree with Sam Harris that in some cases our thought process is forced in a way that reduces our ability to freely make a choice. Brain damage, a tumor, birth defect, trauma, emotional connection, or extreme fear can all take away some degree of our free will. Half of our neural circuitry is wired to take action, and half is wired to inhibit that action. *[Eagleman, 2016]* Imagine if we did whatever we thought of doing, consciously or unconsciously. When the inhibitory parts are impaired, we may do things we know we shouldn't, against our will. But if we have a healthy, fully functional brain, we have what is called *executive function*, or *cognitive control* over our actions, which is the *free will* part, at least as I would define *free will*."

"You make it sound like we have two brains in our heads. Kind of like the little angel and devil who duke it out on your shoulder as they whisper in your ear."

"Kind of, but it's much more complicated than that. The devil is the urge, and the angel is the will. And there are many areas of the brain that attempt to provide their input also. On top of that, we have two kinds of thinking: fast and slow. Fast thinking is intuitive, whereby we follow simple heuristics or rules of thumb to make decisions. We don't think that deeply on most of our decisions, and in these cases, we are not exercising our full power of free will. On the other hand, we are also capable of slow, deliberate thinking that we use for rational problem solving. It is much more methodical, and you might even research more information before making your decision. *[Alcock, 2019, Dual-Process Thinking, and Eagleman, 2016]*

"Sam Harris says if we rewind time and play it forward again under the same circumstances, we would make the same decisions over and over again. How can that be free will?"

"We would freely make the same decisions because nothing has changed in the replay for us to want to make a different choice," Bowtie said. "That is, unless you were aware of the time-rewind thing and were bored and wanted to do something different this time around, but then that would be slightly different circumstances. A physical, non-supernatural version of *free will* doesn't require us to act illogically or randomly. That would be absurd. Free will choices would be anything but random, and random choices would be anything but free will, because our will is based upon our values, information on hand, and some degree of logic."

"HAMBONE ZIPPER!" yelled Greenbeard. "Sorry. It's a habit. Sam Harris says we cannot be held culpable of the choices our brains make, whether it is the result of brain damage or just the way our brains work. There really is no difference between a 'broken' brain or one that just makes bad decisions. Either way, we make the same choices."

"All choices are made with some balance of will and urge. Some people, some of the time, experience uncontrollable urges. But most people, most of the time, make a choice completely within their control, and when they do something immoral or illegal, they do it because they sought personal gain at the expense of others with the intent of getting away with it, or at least not paying society's full price for the crime. Like cheating at a game, or shoplifting. If you lack moral integrity, if you are looking to cheat the social agreement, you should indeed be held culpable for your actions."

"We've never played golf together, have we?" Greenbeard asked.

"I don't believe so," said Bowtie.

"Never mind," said Greenbeard. "But some people have brains that are naturally impulsive. They have a harder time controlling their behavior. How can they be held to the same standard?"

"The criminal will usually control his actions when the likelihood of getting caught is too high. Some who argue that we have no free will go so far as to say that crime should not be punished as we are not responsible for the decisions we make with our deterministic brains. I find that idea a bit insane in itself. The fear of punishment does deter a lot of crime. It is precisely because there are people who are impulsive, inconsiderate, or sociopathic that we need a system of law and order to provide incentive to stay within the acceptable limits of behavior. Sometimes self-discipline is not enough, and we need to impose discipline and judgement upon others."

"We excuse the insane, don't we?" Greenbeard pointed out.

"Insanity is not a reason to excuse someone. Instead it should be taken into consideration of how that person should be dealt with. The insane and dangerously violent offender should simply be permanently removed from society, though in rarer cases, medical treatment can fix the cause of the behavior. But in most cases, we assume a person has enough logical reasoning and self-control that corrective punishment will discourage repeat actions, even with the unrepentant."

"But aren't we still dependent on the information in our brains? Doesn't that ultimately determine our choices? How is that free will?" Greenbeard asked.

Bowtie said: "If we define *free will* as the ability to logically consider the pros and cons of a decision, weigh in on our values, moral or otherwise, and critically think about the consequences of the outcome, then sure, we have free will. If there is no free will, at least in this sense, then there is no such thing as critical thinking."

Seashell jumped in: "Here's the thing: theologians have put forward the idea of free will as a concept whereby we are morally responsible for our actions, and therefore justifiably judged in the end and punished or rewarded. There is no need to abandon the first part of this concept in a secular viewpoint. We have moral values and self-control, and if we do immoral things, we can be justifiably punished for it. Not by a god, but by society. That's how we incentivize good behavior for those who don't find being good for its own sake to be enough."

"Harris says our decisions are handed to us from our subconscious. Brain scans show we make decisions unconsciously, and the experimenters can determine our choice before we are even aware of it ourselves."

"True. But how could we possibly be aware of a decision we have not made yet? There is necessarily an underlying subconscious process that only surfaces in our full awareness after the fact. That doesn't mean that our values and informed opinions were not consulted. Have you ever been asked a trivia question that you couldn't answer right away, and then it came to you a while later? That is your subconscious brain working in the background. Your aware, conscious part of the brain is too busy to do all the work." *[Eagleman, 2016]*

"Ooooh, tell him about his inner zombie," Tortellini said to Bowtie.

Greenbeard jumped and yelled "ZOMBIE!", startling everyone once again. "Sorry. The vodou priest Papa Kanga lives on the other side of the island. Kanga runs Baron Farfalle's farm with zombie slave workers. Scary stuff, really."

"Excuse me," Bowtie interrupted. "Did you say Farfalle?"

"Why yes. Baron Farfalle. Strange fellow. Carries a walking cane with a ruby the size of a golf ball on top." Greenbeard paused a moment as he looked Bowtie up and down. "Kind of looks like you, now that I think of it. But with a goatee."

"And he runs a farm with zombies?" Bowtie asked.

"Yes, the two of them have quite a business going on. Sugar cane I think it is. Or cocaine. Some kind of cane."

"Fascinating. Perhaps we should pay a visit to Baron Farfalle. He's an old acquaintance of mine. But about the zombies: it reminds me of Wade Davis's *The Serpent and the Rainbow*," Bowtie said. "Neurotoxins derived from pufferfish and the plant, *datura,* were reputedly used by Haitian Vodou priests to shut down the conscious part of the victim's brain. That renders the subconscious part of the person, the part that truly lacks free will, as a zombie to do whatever you tell it to do. Same effect as seen in brain-damaged subjects *[Sternberg, 2015]*. There is some controversy to the story, but supposedly the effect ranges from mild suggestibility, similar to the effects of hypnosis, to complete control of the subject. It's a dramatic example of the zombie we all have inside of us."

Greenbeard's eyes popped. "NEPTUNE'S BALLS! Get it out! Get it out!" he yelled.

"Calm down, Mr. Greenbeard," Bowtie said. "It's perfectly normal. Our inner zombie does all the automatic functions, so we don't have to think about them. We couldn't function without it. *[Eagleman, 2016]* A familiar example is when we drive a car while listening to the radio, and suddenly find ourselves miles down the road with no recollection of having driven all that way, navigating intersections and avoiding traffic and pedestrians. Our inner zombie takes over for those things we do on *autopilot*, so to speak. Our brains bypass what we call the *executive function*, the *aware* part of our mind. The zombie mode stores nothing to our episodic memory, where we normally keep track of the various events through the day. We don't remember what our zombie did."

"Now ye be saying we are zombies? I thought you said we have free will?" Greenbeard puzzled.

"We do a lot of things without thinking about them, in which case we don't exercise our free will. Think of it like this. We are all zombies with a special layer on top called self-awareness and cognitive reflection. Our consciousness is reserved for those things we need to cognitively process in our prefrontal cortex, where we do our critical thinking. Our *executive function* is our free-will component which drives the zombie around and makes it do its bidding. At our core we are automatons, but we also have a high degree of free will, or self-determination, in respect to those things that we consciously think about."

"Blow me down!" Greenbeard exclaimed. "I think I savvy. Critical thinking is what gives us free will."

"Or free will is the exercise of critical thinking. The point is, we are highly complex biological machines, so complex that our intricacies will never be fully understood, which makes our brains a kind of magic."

"Oh, ye mean like what me tiny unicorn was telling me?"

"Exactly, albeit nothing supernatural. To call our brains a clockwork mechanism is like comparing the space shuttle to a bottle rocket. We are often unpredictable, and we are highly influenced by emotional response. But we are also capable of very logical, thought-out behavior. This does not run counter to the idea of free will. In fact, it is just the opposite. You want that piece of pie, but you also want your pants to fit. You make the choice to eat it or not based on which you value more, or whether you saw a pleasing drop in the number on the scales that morning. The very fact that belief in free will or the lack thereof can affect your choices shows that we can and do process information and values in our highly complex decision making. Sounds like free will to me."

"So, I don't need to keep blurting out 'BUTT PUSS' to show that I'm in control of my own destiny?"

"Not sure how that would do anything of the kind, actually. How long have you been at this?"

"Oh, about three years, I'd say."

"Why don't you come back with us?"

"Is it my choice?"

"Certainly," said Bowtie.

"What is that in your beard?" Seashell asked. "It smells horrible."

"Don't ask," said Greenbeard.

"Before we go, would you be so kind as to guide us to Farfalle's plantation?" Bowtie asked.

"Baron Farfalle? Are ye sure ye want to go there?"

"He would be very disappointed to learn that I had come by this close and not paid him a visit," Bowtie explained.

"Avast, I will lead ye there, but I won't go near the place." Greenbeard's face turned an even more sickly pale than it already was.

"I will make sure nothing bad happens to you, I promise," Bowtie reassured the pirate. "Please lead the way."

"It suddenly got darker, but I don't see a cloud in the sky," said Greenbeard.

"That was just a bit of literary foreshadowing," Capellini explained.

Greenbeard led Bowtie, Seashell, and Capellini over a volcanic mountain in the middle of the island, while Tortellini, claiming that his bunion was flaring up, waited with the sailors on the beach. After about an hour's walk, the four of them descended into a small valley on the other side of the island. A plantation stretched out before them, surrounding a stately manor home on a small rise which overlooked a rocky beach and a rolling surf. A pier ran out from the shore, upon which the 'cane was piled in bails waiting to be loaded onto a cargo ship.

When they came to the edge of the first field, Greenbeard stopped. "I'll be waiting for ye right here, me hearties. Beware! Papa Kanga deals in black magic, and Baron Farfalle has the evil eye. Some say Kanga captures only your body, but Farfalle captures your soul. Are ye sure you're not related? He looks a mighty lot like ye."

Bowtie simply smiled and continued onward with Seashell and Capellini. They soon passed several laborers dressed in rags and hoeing the rows of plants. The men continued their slow, repetitive hoeing between the plants and did not seem to notice the intrusion of the strangers. They just drooled and stared vacantly ahead, much like the author's office coworkers on a Monday.

As they approached the house, the smell of fresh scones and coffee wafted by. "Ah! Scones! They must be expecting us!" said Capellini, ever the optimist.

"That's just what they want you to think," said Seashell. "I smell a trap."

"Perhaps Baron Farfalle is entertaining guests," suggested Bowtie. "Help me up to that window, Capellini."

Capellini got on all fours and Bowtie stepped up onto his back to peer into the window, which, it being a very pleasant day, was open to allow the gentle breeze off the ocean to flow through the house. Inside he could see a long hall with a conference table running down the middle. At one end was Farfalle, seated in a leather high-backed chair with ornately carved lion-heads on the armrests, and with his cane leaning against his knee. Along either side sat a dozen men in business suits, all turned to look at Farfalle. At the other end of the table sat the one who must be Papa Kanga, in an ice-cream white suit and broad-brimmed hat. A zombie worker in a butler's jacket shuffled slowly behind them, serving scones with a long pair of tongs, and pouring steaming coffee from a silver pot.

"Mr. Kushner," Farfalle said, turning to the man on his left, "Give me an update on our financials."

"It appears we will be finishing out the year with our profits up by eighteen percent over last year," the man said. "Our biggest gains were a result of the shift in tax burden away from corporate revenue and onto future generations."

"Splendid. Trickle down, trickle down, it will. Eventually." Farfalle took a sip of his coffee. "Most of the way, at least. Mr. Gottlieb, were you successful in lifting that pesky drug regulation on heavy metal contamination that was driving up the cost of prescriptions for our dear beloved, hardworking, low-income Americans?"

"Why yes, Baron Farfalle. We simply drafted up a new regulation requiring manufacturers to use easy-to-open pill bottles to allow small children to assist their grandparents in taking their medications. Thanks to the president's new rule requiring us to drop two regulations for every one we impose, we also were able to remove restrictions on testing on chimpanzees."

"Chimpanzees... So useful. Mr. Kushner! Take a note. We need to explore more ways to use chimpanzees. Perhaps they can be used in coal mining. The human workers are getting so expensive, what with treatment for black lung disease and all."

Turning to his right, Farfalle addressed a man in a pinstripe suit. "Mr. Bratva, are we making progress in next year's election cycle?"

"Da, Baron Farfalle. We khev managed to hack into both the Democratic and Republican party servers and inserted extremist initiatives into their planning documents. It is amazing. Once it is in the official party line, they vote for it regardless."

"*Otlichno*, Boris. Did you sneak in the agenda item to require schools to have a separate bathroom for L's, B's, G's, T's and Q's?"

"Of course, Baron Farfalle. With two T's depending on which way they 'T'. We khev even included a bathroom for the asexual of either gender. With the cisgender heterosexual boys and girls, that makes ten separate bathrooms. Coming up with the politically correct door symbols alone will keep them busy for the next five years."

"How sinister of you. Don't forget to require Braille on the toilet handles. And for the Republicans: bibles in every school desk?"

"King James. And blasphemy laws."

Farfalle smiled a wicked smile. "Mr. Wakefield, any new studies published?"

"Tantalizing new evidence of a link between vaccines and delayed potty training."

"Which vaccines?" Farfalle asked.

"All of them," Wakefield replied, shaking his head as if to say *does it even matter*?

Farfalle drummed his fingers on the table. There were some things even *he* found distasteful. "Charles, how are sales of healing crystals and homeopathy products going?"

"Much better now that we have managed to get alternative medicine covered by publicly funded healthcare. The next step is to get them included in our medicinal aid supplies to Africa. What better way to fight HIV, malaria, and hepatitis?"

"Indeed, what better way," mused Farfalle. "Hooper, I understand you have a new proposal to generate more profits in the energy sector?"

"Yes sir." Hooper stood up to begin his presentation. On a large screen behind him there appeared a picture of several bracelets. "This is our new line of energy bracelets. We have recently developed a secretly patented process of putting a frequency into these bracelets that energizes the body and prevents a number of afflictions, such as fibromyalgia, dyspepsia, and Alzheimer's."

"Back up there, Hooper. Is the patent secret, or the process?"

"Both, sir. The patent is registered in the Central Congolese Republic, which was the only country that would take the fee and not ask to actually see the process. The way it works is we insert a frequency into these bracelets that is a harmonic of the earth's natural frequency."

"And how do you insert a frequency? I thought a frequency was just electromagnetic radiation. Something has to emit that frequency."

"Yes, that's the secret part. We pioneered the work last year with these stickers you see on the next slide. You apply them to your arm or chest, and we show they last at least three days, generating about 4.2 Spiesbergers."

"Spiesbergers?"

"Right. A Spiesberger is a unit of energy detectable only with a dowsing rod. With the new process we can supercharge these bracelets and generate on average 72 Spiesbergers, and they last about five years."

"Five years! Very impressive," Farfalle said.

"Well, now," interrupted a bald man halfway down the table, "just how scalable is this? Perhaps we could ramp it up and power a car with these things." Several in the group nodded with interest, wondering if this were possible. "Just imagine, a car which only has to be charged once every five years! We could make a fortune!"

"Sorry gentlemen, that would not work. You see, this technology used in something like a car would violate the first law of Taurocoprology," Hooper explained.[iv]

"The first law? What is that?" the bald man asked.

"Falsifiability is a liability."

"Meaning?" the bald man scowled.

"The car would have to move," said Hooper.

Farfalle rapped his cane on the table. "True, Mr. Hooper. But you can still upscale this without violating the first law. I predict there would be a big market for energy pillows and mattresses."

"Brilliant, sir."

"Hmm. I like it, Mr. Hooper. Let's move ahead with the idea."

"Thank you, sir. I will not let you down."

"Yes, Mr. Hooper. Let us hope that you do not disappoint." Farfalle stood up and began to casually walk around the room.

"Gentlemen, we are on the verge of a new world order. But we must be wary. There are spies everywhere, and several alert conspiracy theorists are onto us. Mr. Pruitt, it appears that you have been seen shifting back and forth from your lizard form. If I receive more reports of this nature, I will find it necessary to *'terminate'* your employment. Do I make myself clear?"

"100 percent, Baron Farfalle. It won't happen again."

Outside, Bowtie felt a tug at his elbow. He looked down from atop Capellini and saw that Greenbeard had caught up with them.

"Mr. Bowtie, I forgot to tell ye. Baron Farfalle has dogs on the grounds. Big ones," Greenbeard said breathlessly.

Bowtie looked toward the corner of the house. A large Rottweiler was staring at the four of them.

Capellini scrambled out from under Bowtie, as Capellini, Greenbeard, and Seashell began to run for a nearby tree. Bowtie found himself hanging in mid-air as the Rottweiler charged. The dog leaped, but Bowtie was abruptly pulled up and through the window, and out of the reach of the snarling, sharp-toothed maw.

"Gentlemen, may I introduce my meddlesome brother, Bowtie." Farfalle let Bowtie fall to the floor with a thud.

"You will never get away with your evil plans," Bowtie declared as he gathered himself together and stood up. "As the Flying Spaghetti Monster is my witness. I will never allow it. My friends are tweeting as we speak, Farfalle. #realBowtie."

"You are mistaken if you think anyone will believe you. Everything you say will be branded as fake news," Farfalle laughed evilly.

Bowtie glanced out the window quickly to see if his friends had gotten away. Greenbeard and Capellini were halfway up the tree, but Seashell knelt at the bottom, feeding the Rottweiler some beef jerky and scratching him behind the ears.

"We are not so different, you and I," smirked Farfalle.

"Well, yeah. Basically, we are the same shape."

"No, I mean that we are both out to change the world, to plant a seed in the mind-space of mankind. We want to change the way people think. Your way of science and critical thinking is really just another way of understanding the world."

"It is the *only* way to understand the world. You promote pseudoscience. It is at best self-deception, and at worst, greedy exploitation of the gullible. I want to bring truth to the world. You bring only lies."

"Seize him, Papa Kanga!" Farfalle called.

Papa Kanga stood up and made ready to grab Bowtie. Bowtie, however, leaped and fell upon Farfalle. The ruby-topped cane flew against the wall and the two tumbled headlong into the butler's service cart. A tray of scones clattered to the ground, and when they stood up again, both pastas sported a goatee.

"Farfalle?" Papa Kanga stared in confusion. "Which one is you?"

"Quick, grab him! He's Bowtie," said the one on the left.

"Don't believe him," said the one on the right. "He's lying."

Papa Kanga thought for a moment. "If Bowtie always tells the truth, and Farfalle always lies, then if you are Farfalle saying he's Bowtie, then that must be a lie and so he is not Bowtie. But if this one is Bowtie then you are telling the truth, and so you can't be Farfalle, ummm, wait a minute."

At this point, the goatee on the right began to droop, the glue not having had time to dry. Bowtie felt his disguise slipping away, and as Papa Kanga's eyes went wide and his mouth curled into an evil smile, Bowtie ran and jumped out the window.

"This way! Run!" he called to Seashell, Capellini, and Greenbeard. They all began to race toward the cover of the coca plants.

Leaning out the window, Farfalle called forward one of his henchmen. "Mr. LaPierre, would you do the honor?"

LaPierre stepped up to the window and drew his model 1911 John Wayne commemorative handgun, which he always kept handy for just such an occasion. Squinting down the barrel, he squeezed the trigger. Greenbeard's head exploded in a fine mist. "Dang. Hit the wrong one," LaPierre said. Before he could squeeze off another shot, Capellini, Seashell, and Bowtie were out of range.

"You should have held your breath when you pulled the trigger," said Farfalle.

"Now is not the time to discuss gun control," LaPierre grumbled. "Let me get my rifle."

"Never mind," said Farfalle as he watched the fleeing figures melt into the green rows of the plantation. "We shall meet again, Bowtie," he muttered as he watched them disappear. "One fine day, we shall meet again."

The Gospel of Peg-Leg Pete

This is the gospel of Peg-Leg Pete, pirate of the high seas who found Bowtie after looking for prophets in all the wrong places.

It were the summer of '04, and I had taken command of the merchant raider *Casanova* sailing under the black flag. Fourteen days out of San Diego, we were cruising the coast of Baja California when we spied a brig bearing the name of *The Naughty Sea Nymph* making for the open seas out of La Paz. She was loaded with boxes marked with top-shelf brands of tequila, PlayStation, and one especially large crate with a Lamborghini symbol on the side. There appeared to be a treasure chest on the aft deck, so brimming with gold doubloons and bejeweled trinkets with rubies the size of walnuts, that the lid would not close. "It's probably so heavy they couldn't carry it below decks," I mused to me cockswain, Robert. With me spyglass I could just make out that her crew consisted of naught but large-breasted ladies who seemed to keep dropping their handkerchiefs and bending over seductively to pick them up. Easy pickings, I thought to me-self. After rousing the boys to a lively sea chantey about rum, booty, and loose women, we began pursuit.

Heading westward into growing swells, we lost sight of the coast, which did not sit well with me men, since I had lost sight of it before on a few occasions when it took some time to find it again. But I had eyes only for the loot, and *The Naughty Sea Nymph* was staying just ahead of us, probably in a hurry to get to Hawaii I speculated, where that crew of curvaceous women would frolic on the beach under the palm trees in floral bikinis.

The ladies coyly played hard-to-get, staying just ahead of us. After several hours, the winds slackened, and the *Nymph* slowed its pace. We finally gained on her. Me first mate, also named Robert, made ready with the grappling hooks as we pulled up alongside the ship, and I called out something clever like "Permission to come aboard, me ladies?" which was funny since we had every intention to board, permission or no, and there just might be a little sexual innuendo in there, if you know what I mean.

It was then that I noticed one of the crew on the *Nymph* wearing a cute little orange sundress seemed to be sporting a beard. In fact, a number of them did. Two of the bearded ladies approached the Lamborghini crate and began to open it with crowbars. Now I fully expected to see a beautiful yellow sports car, perhaps presented here as a sacrificial offering from the ladies wishing to preserve their virginity.

But much to my surprise, it were not a sports car, but a Gatling gun. "Avast," I called to Robert, me first mate, not the cockswain. "Could this be a trap?"

Before my equally confused mate could respond, the very gates of Hell seemed to open up, and in a typhoon of splinters and molten lead, the deck of me ship was soon razed. Being a quick thinker, I had taken cover behind a heavy oak barrel of after-shave. We had taken a blast below the water line and began to list to larboard. Our cannon, loosed in ready for our attack, rolled with the inclining deck and sealed our fate. The tilt further exposed our hull to the *Nymph's* guns which made Swiss cheese out of us. We were going down fast.

I gave the order to abandon ship, and those of us still alive cut loose the dinghies and climbed in. It were naught but two minutes before we saw the last of the *Casanova* sink beneath the waves. The crew of the *Nymph* jeered at us as they took off wigs and bonnets. I began to doubt there was even a lady among them. They soon changed tack and headed back to land, leaving us to the sharks.

We were adrift for many days. Fortunately, we had taken on a fresh supply of cabin boys out of San Diego, so we were not to starve, but our casks of fresh water would soon run out, and by day three I had to order the men to stop using it for bathing, which caused some grumbling among them. T'were understandable, as the body odor in close quarters was at times a bit stiff.

The winds at this latitude prevailed out of the east, causing us to drift toward the very heart of the Pacific, into the doldrums as it were. It were both a curse and a blessing that we were not hit by a gale, as our little boat would have been swamped with the first big wave, but the sun beat down with an unbearable heat, and my sunscreen had run out by the tenth day. By day twelve I was ready to kill Robert, the cockswain, not the first mate, when he joked for the hundredth time about how he knew I was into sailing, because some girl told him that I had a little dinghy.

Adrift in the middle of the vast ocean, I had plenty of time to me thoughts. Perhaps I should have seen it coming. Was I blind to the clues? Was I seeing only what I wanted to see? Could I be at fault for the loss of me ship? Me forkscrew was causing me a great deal of pain. I should have been more wary, as the Nymph was indeed a *hermaphrodite* brig, which is funny, you see, my joke being that *hermaphrodite* is a biological term for animals or plants possessing both male and female genitalia, and a hermaphrodite brig is a brig having one mast with square sails and a second mast with gaff and triangular sail like a schooner. A regular brig has two masts with all square sails. My pun here is really quite clever if you think about it.

By day forty, we were down to a thimble full of water and the last cabin boy. His name, the cabin boy, was Robert, too. His head looked like it had been taken apart and put back together wrong. Robert, the first mate, not the cockswain, was so painfully blistered with sunburn that I feared he would be dead before dusk. I took up me spyglass to scan the horizon yet again for any sign of a passing ship. Turning it to the northwest, I saw some gulls and then, much to my surprise, made out a thin brown line stretching north to south. Me map showed only *here be dragons*, thar being no known islands in the vicinity.

"Land ho!" I cried. We put oars in the water and made way toward the spot. Soon the sky was teeming with gulls. As we neared the island, the water became thick with debris. I dipped out a cupful and examined it, finding it to be bits of plastic.

When we reached the island itself, we stepped ashore onto a softly undulating substrate of refuse. It were all made of plastic, far as the eye could see. There were plastic grocery bags, candy wrappers, Tupperware® bowls, Chinese take-out containers, margarine container lids, K-cups®, egg cartons, fortune cookie wrappers with the fortune cookies still in them, coffee stirs, single-serving coffee creamer containers, fast-food cups, fast-food cup holders, frozen veggie bags, toy action figures and Barbie dolls with missing arms, Barbie shoes, Barbie convertibles, nylon fishing line, plastic forks, spoons, and knives, some of them still individually wrapped with a napkin and salt and pepper packs, plastic plates, extra-thick vacuum-formed product packaging that you have to saw through to open the damn thing, plastic clothes pins, potato chip bags, potato chip bag clips, Tic-tac® dispensers, cheese stick wrappers, ketchup bottles, ketchup packets, squeaky dog toys, sex toys, squeaky dog-sex toys, cat litter buckets, shampoo bottles, detergent bottles, milk bottles, Amazon® air pillows for packing boxes, delivery pizza savers to keep the cheese off the lid, red and blue beer cups, zip-lock® sandwich bags, plastic straws, and individual wrappers for plastic straws.

Disgusting as it were, we were glad to set foot on semi-solid ground. We began to make our way inland, where the plastic was denser and more fused together, and piled into mounds higher than our heads. The first hut we came across was made of PVC pipe and plastic sheeting. We knocked on the door and a little old man with a grizzled beard poked his head out. "How can I help ye?" he asked.

"I am the dreaded pirate Peg-leg Pete," I answered. I always found it best to begin with a little intimidation, just to set the tone.

"Dreaded pirate, are ye?" he said. "We all are dreaded pirates here, so you can stow the attitude."

I looked aside at Robert, me first mate, not the cockswain, wondering what kind of a character we had stumbled upon.

"It don't look like ye have a peg leg," he added.

"Well, that's just the name the ladies gave me. The *third leg*, if ye know what I mean," I replied.

"I don't think they meant that as a compliment," he said.

"I believe ye've missed the implication that a peg is made of hard wood, my good sir," I explained.

"Well, Peg-head, state yer business," he said.

"What be the name of this island?" I inquired.

"Name? It don't have none that I know of," he said. "And it's not so much an island as a floating pile of trash. Size of Texas, it is."

"Is there anyone else living here?" I asked.

"Oh, 'bout thirty thousand of us, I reckon. All pirates who washed ashore at some point or other. The city is about fifteen miles that way," he said, pointing toward the west.

We were a bit taken aback at this news. Thirty thousand men living here? In the middle of the Pacific? We had a million questions. Is there beer? Rum? Harlots? Girlie magazines? But our immediate needs were ones of survival.

"Might ye have some water and sunscreen to spare?" I asked.

"Oh, the dreaded pirate needs some help? In a bit of a bind, are we?" He shook his head, disappeared inside for a moment, and returned with an old Cool Whip® container full of rainwater, and a couple tubes of partially used Chapstick. "Chapstick's the best I have to offer. These things wash ashore all the time. Never seen an empty one," he said more to himself than to us as he handed them over.

"Thank you for your hospitality, good sir," I said. "Fifteen miles that way?"

"You see that giant pile of Styrofoam take-out boxes? Head in that direction and keep the setting sun in front of you. Ya're getting close when you start to see piles of poop everywhere. That's why I live clear out here. No sewer system for the next 300 miles."

"Sounds charming," I said. We slaked our thirst, applied some Chapstick, and prepared to head out.

We walked for several hours until the sun set, and camped in a glade of tampon applicators. We were hungry and had been collecting bits of dried rice and French fries from food containers as we went. We soaked it in some standing rainwater and greedily wolfed it down before we settled in for the night. Robert, the cockswain, had found some packets of ketchup, but he wasn't sharing. There arose a disagreement among the men about whether it was spelled *catsup* or *ketchup*, and it took some time to convince the men that both were acceptable, even though it only said *ketchup* on the packets. The next morning, we arose and continued our journey without breakfast.

About noon we started to notice the piles of poop here and there, becoming more and more unavoidable. I feared me new Tommy Hilfiger deck shoes would be ruined. Ahead of us the mounds of plastic rubbish began to take on more structured shapes, and we began to make out people walking between them. As we got closer, we could see there were houses, water towers, office buildings, banks, saloons, park benches, statues, and even a stadium, all built from plastic trash. In the parks there were green trees, which upon closer examination turned out to be made of plastic water bottles and covered with a fine moss, which grew in various places on the island, it being a humid latitude. There were electricity lines strung about, and just outside of town we could smell the power station, burning rubbish to run the generators. A whole pirate civilization had been built upon the discarded refuse of humanity. A somewhat clear path through the poop led us to a grand avenue that passed through the heart of the city.

We stopped a man with a newspaper under his arm walking in the opposite direction and asked where we might find a good meal and a bed for the night. He spoke with such a thick Cornish accent that even we, being experienced pirates and all, had a harrrhd time understanding him. We were directed to an inn called *the Bucket and Baggie*. The inn was serving turtle soup, which we were soon to learn was a staple for the locals, as the turtles washed ashore all the time after they choked to death on plastic bags which in the water closely resemble their usual food, jelly fish. The owner had us try a house specialty of his own invention, which he called moss cheese, which was cheese, made from moss. He was quite proud of it, but I thought it tasted more like moss than cheese.

After we had finished our meal, our thoughts turned to other matters. I asked the innkeeper how long he had been stranded here.

"Stranded?" the inn-keeper replied, "Who be stranded here? We can catch the next ship out at any time."

"Next ship?" I replied. "We can sail home at any time? Why would thirty thousand pirates live on a floating trash heap if they could just sail back to the mainland whenever they want?"

"No corporate taxes," the innkeeper said. "Of course, we have no sewer system either. But here we live the pirate's dream. No taxes, no government interference in our private affairs."

"Avast," I said, "Sounds like Republicans."

"Blimey, mate," said the innkeeper, "The Republican party were founded by pirates!"

"Founded by pirates? Ye be telling me the Republicans are descended from pirates?"

"Yarh, I thought everyone knew that," he said. "Think about it, mate. Hostile takeovers. They bury their treasure offshore."

It struck me like a jolt of Saint Elmo's fire. "Well, now that I think about it, it all makes sense. They have about the same view on women's rights and executive compensation," I said.

"Aye, and gun laws," added Robert.

And the other Robert chimed in: "Everyone knows the only thing that can stop a good pirate with a blunderbuss is a bad pirate with a blunderbuss."

"I thought it was the other way round," I said.

"Depends which side you're on," Robert replied.

"And if they can shut down the EPA and disband the national park service, the country will look a lot like this place," said Robert, the cabin boy.

"Still, it be a bit strange that the Republicans are descended from free-thinking pirates, what with their ties to the Christian right and all," I said.

"Yarhhh," said the innkeeper. "They do make strange bedfellows."

"Well then, when is the next ship out?" I inquired.

"The *Scarlet Avenger* should be ready to hoist anchor in a few days," he said.

"Aye, a few days. So, me crew be looking for some recreation hereabouts. What passes for entertainment?" I asked.

"Mostly we play *go-fish* and dance to accordion music."

We had truly landed in the bowels of Hell, methought.

"Every other weekend we put on a burlesque show. Micky Grimwald is not too shabby looking in drag when he shaves his beard," said the innkeeper. "Late September we hold a shark rodeo. Should be a bug-eating contest tonight down at *Le Poubelle Chat*."

"Be thar anything for more refined tastes?" I asked with a wink, implying that perhaps there might be an establishment where the ladies are cordial and the whiskey does not taste of dirty socks.

"If ye be into sermons ye can go listen to Bowtie. He has been preaching out on the Mount of Beerbottles most evenings. Free pizza and beer to anyone who listens."

The innkeeper had apparently missed my inuendo. "Bowtie?" I wondered, raising me eyebrows. "Never heard of him."

"Ye have never heard of the living son of the Flying Spaghetti Monster?" he said, a bit astonished. "He's converted nearly the whole island to Pastafarianism. Thar be probably twenty thousand pirates here who have taken up the colander and follow Bowtie." He held up the tiny colander hanging on a chain around his neck.

"Colander? Why the colander?" I asked.

"Yarh, I'm curious meself," thought the innkeeper. "Seems every time we bring it up, he doesn't want to talk about it. Anyhow, thar be many who say Bowtie is a noodle of great wisdom, so ye might want to give him a listen."

"What do ye say, mates?" I looked around.

"Sure, why not," said Robert, the cockswain, not the first mate.

"Count me in," said Robert, the first mate, not the cockswain.

"Aye," said Robert, the cabin boy.

And so the next evening, me crew and I made our way to just outside of town where the Mount of Beerbottles towered slightly above the surrounding Plain of Mayonnaise Jars. I would not exactly call the crowd a throng. It was just me and Robert the cockswain, Robert the first mate, Robert the cabin boy, Ziggy our fashion coordinator, Jackknife Willie our ship's doctor, and Bob the cook. Bowtie and his helpers, Rigatoni and Linguine, didn't show up until half an hour later and almost seemed surprised to see anyone had shown up. For a son of divine origin, Bowtie didn't appear to be anything out of the ordinary, I mean other than the fact that he was a walking, talking, bow-tie shaped piece of pasta with rolling eyes like Thomas the Tank Engine.

"You must be getting hungry," said Linguine. And that was when we witnessed the miracle of the pizza and beer. He placed before us a pizza box and opened the lid. Inside we saw the pizza had been cut into six slices.

"But there are seven of us," I pointed out. "One of us will have to go without a slice."

Linguine smiled and turned the box around so the lid blocked our view. He reached in and handed a slice to Robert, Robert, Ziggy, Robert, Jackknife Willie, and Bob. Six slices handed out and I still had none. Then he reached in and pulled out a seventh slice and handed it to me. It was delicious, though I had to pick off the green pepper. "Blimey! How did you do that?" I wondered.

"How come mine and Ziggy's are smaller?" Bob complained.

"You must be getting thirsty," said Rigatoni as he opened the cooler he had carried with him, and in it we saw a six-pack of beer.

"But there are seven of us," I cried. "One of us will have to go without a beer."

Rigatoni smiled as he closed the lid of the cooler, then opened it again, and pulled out a cold beer, handing it to Bob. He then did the same for Ziggy, Jackknife Willie, Robert, Robert, and Robert. I was on edge now, because that had to be the last one, I thought. Then Rigatoni opened the cooler and pulled out a seventh beer. "Shiver me timbers!" I said, taking the frosty cold beer. I popped it open, and it was not too bad. A little too much hops I thought. "Surely this is a miracle!"

Then Bowtie stepped up on the mount and looked down on us. And he began thusly:

"*Praised are the critical thinkers, for by reducing bias, they shall come closest to the truth.*"

"*Praised are the moderators, for through thoughtful debate and exchange of ideas, we can reach mutual agreement instead of fighting like children.*"

"*Praised are the sober, for they will drive us home safely.*"

"*Faith is a false virtue. There is nothing virtuous about not requiring evidence to believe something.*"

"*In the past it was said: Remain unwavering in your convictions. But I say unto you, be swayed by a solid argument. If logic and facts disagree with you, just admit you were wrong.*"

"*Embrace being wrong, for in the realization, you become wise.*"

I could see there was a theme here, I thought to meself.

"*Everyone has their own version of Truth, with a capital T. But I say instead seek truth with a small t, as truth is reality, and in it we find a greater beauty and understanding.*"

"*Don't jump to the supernatural explanation but seek answers in the more mundane. Things are weirder than they seem, but not that weird.*"

"Life, and everything in it, is complicated. If you think you know all about something, it is more likely that you know too little about it to grasp how much you don't know. It's called the Dunning-Kruger effect. Ignorance breeds overconfidence."

"Jesus is not the answer for all the world's problems. Birth control is, at least for most of them."

Bowtie took yet another beer out of the cooler, cracked it open and took a sip. Linguine and Rigatoni then did the same. That was ten bottles out of a cooler that only held six beers. I was so flabbergasted that I missed the next couple of things Bowtie said, but I am sure they were good and wise. The next I can remember was this one:

"If you disagree with the overwhelming scientific consensus, and you don't have an advanced degree in the field, you are wrong. Period. Just shut up and stop embarrassing yourself."

"When an issue is scientific, listen to the scientists, not the politicians and pundits. When sides of an issue divide down political lines, the public debate is mostly irrational and tribalistic."

"Don't assume that because the other party champions an issue, it is wrong. Let a claim stand on its logical merit, not on who said it, even if it was Al Gore."

"Vote. Get off your ass, read up on the issues and candidates, and vote. Don't say you are not interested in politics. That's like saying you're not interested in looking out the window when you are driving the car."

It was as though Bowtie looked through my soul at that moment. I had intended to vote in the last election, but it was happy hour at the Dog and Partridge, and my darts team was in the next round.

"Freedom does not mean freedom to be a dick. Or a bigot. Especially religious freedom."

"Life is not fair. But you should be."

"Do not take comfort in the idea that the universe is unfolding as it should. Really bad things happen to good people, and good things happen to really bad people. Instead, take comfort in the fact that you are not alone. If we all work together, peace, love, and justice, for the most part, will prevail."

"Don't take my word for it. Think about it. Analyze, criticize, theorize. Postulate, contemplate, evaluate."

And Bowtie said so many other wonderful things, some of which we lacked human words for and had to be written in Klingon, but I seem to have lost those notes.

By the end of Bowtie's sermon, the pizza and beer had run out. I guess a magic cooler only goes so far. So, we headed into town for some grog and moss cheese.

Two days later me and Robert, the first mate, not the cockswain, signed on with the *Scarlet Avenger* and set sail for New Jersey, and as luck would have it, Bowtie and his A-Pastas joined us, the audiences having dried up of late. On the voyage Tortellini baptized me in olive oil and I became a Bowtian.

Bowtie taught me many things about reality-based thinking, and it was as though the scales fell from my eyes. He was truly the son of the Flying Spaghetti Monster. I swear upon my testicles.

Unfortunately, upon our arrival in America, a crowd of drunken Pastafarians and sober evangelical Christians cornered Bowtie in the port parking lot, where they boiled him and ate him. Bowtie did not rise up from the dead ever again. It was just as the prophecy said.

I myself then traveled far and wide with the A-Pastas, learning the ways of the noodley master and preaching the good word, until I met a girl named Misty in a karaoke bar and we settled down together in a town outside Raleigh.

The Unnatural Acts of the A-Pastas

After the death of Bowtie and his subsequent non-resurrection, the A-Pastas realized that they needed to generate some income without the popular draw of Bowtie. Manicotti suggested that perhaps one of them could dress up as Bowtie and try to pass himself off as the *One True Son*® of the Flying Spaghetti Monster, but Elbow nearly killed himself trying to tie his body into a bowtie shape and soon the effort was abandoned.

Even without Bowtie, the flame had been lit. People came from far and wide to hear the amazing things the A-Pastas had to say about the new and everlasting divine non-aggression pact Bowtie had arranged to keep everybody out of eternal punishment without having to wear an eye patch. But some questioned the veracity of Bowtie's claim to being the son of a deity, a claim which rested upon the fact that Bowtie did not rise from the dead. The A-Pastas quickly put this to rest, citing the precedent set by Jesus, who's claim to divine-offspring status just as logically rested on an unverifiable empty tomb.

Not all received the word of Bowtie without challenge, which was good, as it showed they were at least questioning the awesome word of the one true legitimate son of the Flying Spaghetti Monster and not blindly accepting the word of strangers. Now it cannot be said that Bowtie's words were awesome because he was a *legitimate* son, as that would seem to imply that persons born out of wedlock are somehow lesser beings, and this is certainly not the case, and this disgraceful term should be retired, and we should consider every living being as legitimate. Awesomeness stands on its own and does not depend upon parental lineage or marital status. And we hope the reader also finds his words to be awesome. No one wants to read mediocre scripture. Right, Mormons?

And behold, the multitudes gathered to hear the word of Bowtie. It came to pass that when the A-Pastas explained how science was leaving less and less space for the 'God of the Gaps', and by implication, more and more room for the Flying Spaghetti Monster, who never minded the gaps, one objector in the multitude threw out the argument from order: "But surely the universe would be nothing but chaos if there were no omnipotent God keeping things running like clockwork."

Tortellini fielded this one with these words: "The universe is indeed chaotic, and in just the way a Flying Spaghetti Monster might leave it. There are planet-sterilizing death rays emanating from the poles of collapsed stars. Supernovas wipe out anything near them. Asteroids and comets have hit the earth regularly in the past, causing great devastation. It's a very dangerous place and the vast majority of the universe is uninhabitable, even by extremophile microbes. Everything is floating around higgledy-piggledy out there in space, and things smash into each other all the time. Look at the craters on the moon for the evidence. But our noodley master leaves his mark to show us he is there: every so often the moon turns red to remind us of a great tomato sauce covered meatball."

A woman in the crowd shouted back, "But what about the way we can mathematically describe the universe, and the way we can precisely and repeatedly observe the laws of nature? Surely an intelligent designer must have created these laws!"

"What else would you expect from a natural world?" replied Tortellini. "If physics did not work the same way every time, the universe would have to keep making things up. It would have to be much more creative. We don't see gravity changing its mind and push in the other direction now and then. The speed of light doesn't slow down on Mars or speed up in the Andromeda Galaxy. A universe which *didn't* obey natural and unchanging laws would be suggestive of an energetic divine creator rather than a Flying Spaghetti Monster who would rather leave things as they are and enjoy a beer instead."

Another in the crowd threw out the argument from fine tuning, "Physics shows that the fundamental structure of the universe is precisely tuned. If there were even a small change in the weight of a proton, or the acceleration of gravity, things would be very different. The universe would not support life as we know it. Doesn't that imply an intelligent designer?"

Vermicelli answered, "A Flying Spaghetti Monster might be spewing millions of un-tuned universes into existence with his bubble machine. Most of the bubble universes collapse or pop, but a very few might stick around long enough, and with just the right qualities that in some remote corners of them, perhaps on an obscure planet circling an average star on the spiral arm of an insignificant galaxy, you find beings capable of debating the existence of gods. And life as we know it does not include all the variations of life as it could possibly be."

An Amish farmer stepped forward and taking the stalk of wheat he had been chewing on out of his mouth said, "But isn't that an example of *abductive reasoning*, which means it can't be used to logically argue the point?"

Vermicelli puzzled. "Abductive reasoning?"

"You know," the farmer explained, "it's where we observe A but can't explain it, so we hypothesize that if B were true, it would cause A, therefore we conclude B must be true. But that is a logical fallacy, as there may be other explanations for A, and there is no corroborative evidence for B." He stuck the stalk of wheat between his teeth and turned to the man next to him saying "At least that's what we say back on the farm."

"True," Vermicelli conceded. "I'm not saying there actually *are* infinite bubble universes popping into existence. I'm offering it as an alternative and just as likely a cause for the universe we see to counter the abductive reasoning that person over there just used for the existence of an intelligent designer."

"Touché", said the Amish farmer. "Fair enough."

Still another shouted above the crowd, "But what about all the beautiful religious paintings, crucifixes, stained glass, all the time spent praising God, all the wars defending the faith, all the martyrs who gave their lives? You can't say it was all a waste! How can you just turn your back on the sacrifice of Jesus?"

Seashell spoke up in answer: "It's bad logic to assume something must be true because people have put so much effort into it. That's called the *sunken cost* fallacy. You already believe that all the work that went into temples and carvings for Shiva, and tributes and sacrifices for Jupiter and Zeus and Poseidon were for nothing. No matter how much effort and hope you put into your faith, it does not make it any *truer*. Reality doesn't work that way. But remember, the Flying Spaghetti Monster asks nothing of you, so no harm, no foul."

"But it is virtuous to believe," said another. "Truly, our reward will be great if our faith is strong. Even more so without evidence. Jesus said to doubting Thomas: '*Because you have seen me, you have believed; blessed are those who have not seen and yet have believed.*'"

Manicotti took his turn: "Why is it less virtuous to believe in the words of Muhammed? Why is it not just as good to believe in Vishnu, or Thor? Believing without requiring evidence says you don't care if it is true or not. Then it is not so much belief as just pretending. And in that case, you might as well pretend to believe in the Flying Spaghetti Monster."

The crowd murmured as it mulled this over.

Then, from the back of the crowd, a fundamentalist preacher spoke up and everyone turned around to see who was speaking. "But if man evolved from apes," he said, "then why are there still apes?"

A hushed silence spread over the crowd as the A-Pastas looked at each other for a stunned moment.

"WHAT ARE YOU, AN IDIOT?" Couscous replied.ᵛ

And so, many people sold all their belongings and joined the cult of Bowtie.

"It's not a cult," insisted Tortellini.

I'm sorry. I didn't know you could hear the narrator, said the narrator. But it was a lot like a cult in that people cashed in all their earthly possessions and gave the money to the A-Pastas and lived communally with flowers in their hair, but less like a cult in that they weren't cut off from family members or shunned from society when they showed some independent thinking, unlike Jehovah's Witnesses, or Mormons. In fact, the majority of the new converts had almost nothing to sell anyway, and a lot of them just thought they were getting away with free room and board, and the possibility of some groovy casual commune sex.

One day in the commune, Fettuccini told the story of how Bowtie tried to pick figs out of season from the neighbor's yard, and when he couldn't find any, he got angry and cursed the tree, blaming it for not producing fruit. The next day, the tree was withered and dead. *[Matt 21:19]*

"Oh, I get it, Tortellini pointed out to Fettuccini, "Bowtie was using the tree as a metaphor for what happens to church members who don't give us all their money," he said, thinking of that couple who said they sold their house for 500 schmeckels, even though Seashell saw the property transfer in the paper, settling the deal at 700 schmeckels. "Just like what happened back in Camden," he said.

"What! No! I tell you those people just fell over dead," Fettuccini insisted. "I had nothing to do with it!"

"But as you were arguing and the guy was insisting it was 500 schmeckels, he falls over dead. You and Vermicelli took his body out back, then his wife comes in and you don't even tell her that her husband has died. Instead you ask her about the money, and she says, yeah, sure, it was 500 schmeckels, and then she keels over dead too. And she had the extra 200 schmeckels in her purse which you rummaged through. You're telling me that was just a coincidence?" *(Yes, that really happens in Acts 5:1.)*

"Look, what happens in Camden stays in Camden," Vermicelli said.

The narrator looked the other way.

Actually, the story of the fig tree in Matthew was told to say that if you believe hard enough, you too can make fig trees wither, and make mountains fly into the sea. Good luck with that. Bowtie had to use Round-up to pull off that trick. As Jesus's apostles learned, sometimes, like with the new converts falling over dead and pilfering the money out of their purse, you have to take matters into your own hands. But if Bowtie were still around, he would be quite horror-struck at what Fettuccini and Vermicelli had done, as I am sure Jesus would have been had he seen how things played out after he died.

After that, the A-Pastas set out for the four corners of the world, assuming it was flat and not as big as it turned out to be, to evangelize with the good word of Bowtie. One day, at Eddie's barber shop in Perth Amboy, the disciples Manicotti, Fettuccini and Vermicelli stopped in for a haircut.

"What'll it be?" Eddie asked Vermicelli, who was the first to settle into the chair.

"Oh, the lambchops are getting bushy, and if you could get the back of my neck, please."

"Yeah, he's starting to look like sasquatch back there," said Manicotti.

"So, what have you boys been up to lately," asked Eddy as he fired up his shears.

"Well, we've been traveling the countryside, spreading the good news of Bowtie," Vermicelli replied.

"Bowtie? You mean that guy on TV who teaches science to kids?" Eddie asked.

"Nah! You're thinking of Bill Nye. I'm talking about Bowtie, the son of the Flying Spaghetti Monster. He was eaten by an angry mob a while back and he never rose again, just like he prophesized. So, we travel all over, telling his stories and doing miracles with a deck of cards and the occasional three-card monte."

"Stories?"

"Yeah, mostly philosophical stories about how to be a better person, and why science is the best approximation of the truth, way better than relying on late-bronze-age metaphysical concepts."

"What is your favorite Bowtie story?" Fettuccini asked Vermicelli.

"Well, the best ones are where he said things that were so marvelous that there aren't real words to write them down," Vermicelli said, alluding to Third Nephi 19:34 of the Book of Mormon, where Jesus does just this when he visits the Jewish tribes of Nephites and Lamanites in pre-Columbian America and fills them with the love and grace of the holy spirit for a few years before they all turn bad again and kill each other by the millions.

"But I would have to say my favorite is Bowtie's story about the tunnel at the end of the light."

"You mean *the light at the end of the tunnel*?" Eddie interrupted, as a large ball of neck hair rolled down Vermicelli's back and onto the floor.

"Eddie, you cut, I talk," Vermicelli said.

He began: "It was back in Palermo, where we camped on the beach during the spring break of '82 ..." At this point the barbershop morphed into squiggly lines and a beach appeared.

"*If I'm not back again this time tomorrow,*" Capellini sang as he plucked out Bohemian Rhapsody on a ukulele. "*Carry on, carry on as if nothing really matters.*" The driftwood fire crackled in the twilight as the gentle waves rhythmically washed ashore. The A-pastas were settling down to beers and oysters, and a welcome break from the daily grind of proselytizing.

"I could go for a pizza," said Rigatoni, not implying that he would actually go to pick up a pizza, having no money, but that if there were a pizza around, he would certainly be willing to partake in it.

"Where is Ziti?" Ravioli asked as he cracked open a beer and looked around for his cousin who had joined them for the weekend.

"He was looking pretty wasted, last I saw," said Penne. "Said something about taking a swim."

"But he can't swim!" Ravioli began to worry. "He'll just get soft and limp in the water."

"*I see a little silhouetto of a man, Scaramouch, Scaramouch, will you do the Fandango?*"

Ravioli and Penne stood up and began looking up and down the beach for any sign of Ziti. Just then, a young girl about fifty yards away screamed. "He's dead!" she cried. Ravioli and Penne began to run toward the girl, soon followed by Tortellini and Rigatoni.

"What is it?" Penne called to the girl. "What do you see?"

"It's a jellyfish," she said, pointing to an enormous Portuguese man-o-war that had washed up on the sand. "There, beside that limp piece of pasta."

"Ziti!" Ravioli yelled, and ran to kneel by his cousin, being careful not to touch the gelatinous mass of the stinking jellyfish. It was too late. Ziti, soggy and limp like a noodle, was dead.

"Ziti! Why? Why oh Flying Spaghetti Monster? Why did you take him from me? Oh, Death, you cruel, cruel reaper." Ravioli broke down in heaving sobs. Soon, a crowd began to gather, wondering what the big deal was, and some started to poke the jellyfish with a stick.

Bowtie approached and looked down on the deceased Ziti. "You know, this reminds me of a sermon I once gave," he began, as the other A-pastas gathered round.

"*Galileo, Galileo, Figaro, Magnifico – oh -oh...*"

"Put that ukulele down and come over here, Capellini," Bowtie called.

"Is that Ziti?" Capellini asked. "He looks dead!"

Once everyone had gathered, Bowtie asked: "What is death?"

For a few moments the only sound was the rush of waves onto the shore.

"Death is..." Couscous said and thought a moment. "Death is... is... a flower."

"Shut up, Couscous," Tortellini admonished.

"Death is a passage to a better place," Elbow offered. "That's why we say someone passed on."

"But they didn't pass on," Bowtie said. "They died. Expired. *Finito*."

A seagull shrieked as it squabbled with a ragged looking albatross over a fish.

"I don't think it is healthy to pretend that death is not real. Couscous was on to something with the flower idea. Life is a flower that blossoms and eventually fades, leaving behind only seeds to show that it was ever there." Couscous smiled smugly and burped.

Bowtie continued: "But we like to imagine that death, rather than being an end of life, is a passage to another place. And what makes you think that place, a place for which there is simply no evidence, is better?"

"This can't be all there is to life. I have to believe there is more than this, that there is a light at the end of the tunnel," Elbow said.

"You are implying that we are in a tunnel right now, and a pretty dismal one," Bowtie said. "I tell you, we are not in a tunnel, and you are not heading toward the light, but rather you are already in the light."

"What light is that?" Manicotti inquired, looking down at the pale face of the lifeless Ziti. He took a long swallow of his beer.

"You are in the light of consciousness. Your brain is the product of more than thirteen billion years of the unfolding of the universe, the forging of elements in the stars, the explosions of supernovas. Over the course of four billion years of chemistry and evolution on this planet, from bacteria to complex cells, to tissues and nervous systems, our humble earth gave birth to the self-aware brain that ultimately lets you, a sentient being, look around and ponder the wonders of existence."

"But surely consciousness goes beyond this life!" Elbow said. "No one can explain consciousness. It must come from the other side, the spiritual world."

"That would be your tiny unicorn talking," said Bowtie. "If you consider the gradual development of the brain from very basic animals with rudimentary response to stimuli, such as the sea cucumber, to fully responsive but unreflective fish and reptiles, to fully conscious birds and mammals with distinct personalities, to self-aware and self-reflective humans and other intelligent species, you will find a gradual progression of a layered neural system which ultimately lets us look inward as well as outward. Despite the deep debate of the exact nature of the conscious experience, we actually do have a pretty good understanding of how consciousness arises in a fully material world. Read the works of Daniel Dennett and others. They don't all agree on every aspect, but they do provide a solid basis for understanding consciousness. The problem is that it takes a lot of time and effort which a lot of us will never invest."

Elbow turned his head to the side, trying to hush the little unicorn whispering in his ear.

"Just because some will throw up their hands and say it is inconceivable does not mean that magic is the answer. There are many things that are very difficult to understand, and they boggle our minds. Most people can't fathom the size of the universe or comprehend cellular biology. But that does not make the universe any smaller, or photosynthesis any simpler. It all comes down to this: we can explain consciousness as a function of the brain, and we have no reason to expect that consciousness can continue without the brain. Every night when we fall asleep, we spend hours in a state of nothingness. We know that consciousness is completely suspended when normal brain function is chemically stopped through anesthesia, to the point that we don't even react to the removal of major organs. All we experience is a gap in time. In fact, we don't even experience that. We simply wake up in what we perceive to be the next moment, even though hours may have passed. That is true death."

Elbow frowned. "If we are in the light now, what do we have to look forward to when we enter the tunnel? We spend billions of years waiting to come along, and life lasts the blink of an eye? Such a brief moment in the crack of light, and all we have to look forward to is an eternity of darkness? Nothing but endless billions of years in the tunnel at the end of the light?"

"Well, that would be pretty dismal if we were a wisp of consciousness floating through a dark eternity. But that is not how it works, Elbow. The truth is that there is only the light," Bowtie explained. "There is no tunnel at the end of it. Your alpha and omega, all that you will ever know, your entire eternity, as far as you are concerned, is the light of this life. There is only the path from your birth to your death, and nothing beyond. Just as there was no you before you were born, there will be no you after you are gone. But you will never know that time before or after. You live only in the light. You don't mourn or even miss the time you were dead for all those billions of years before you were born, and neither shall you mind being dead for billions of years into the future. It is only right now, while you are alive, that you experience the angst of one day being dead, and it is a shame that we spend so much of our valuable living time fretting about the day when we are no longer here."

"I SEE DEAD PEOPLE," Couscous said.

"Yes, we all do, Couscous," said Seashell. "It's Ziti."

"BUT THEY CAN'T SEE ME!" Couscous said.

"Don't think of it as dust to dust, but rather as life, just life. Nothing else. Seize the day! You are alive now! Enjoy it."

"But when people have come back from death, they talk about seeing a light at the end of a tunnel! How can that be if there is no tunnel?" Elbow asked.

"What we call a near-death experience is actually a brain process that happens when deprived of oxygen," Bowtie explained. "Although there are many stories of people witnessing things they could not possibly have seen or heard if they had not left their bodies, upon close examination the stories either fall apart or are unverifiable. These people are convinced they left their bodies, and it makes for fascinating stories that get embellished and passed on. But they always fall short of real evidence."

"What are they seeing, then?" Elbow asked.

"When the brain begins to shut down from lack of oxygen, one gets tunnel vision, where peripheral vision is grayed out. Just ask any fighter pilot what it is like to pull so many G's that the blood drains from their brain. The person may experience hallucinations. If we really departed from our brains, then we would not have any memories of it, being that memories are physically stored in the brain. Out-of-body sensations and near-death experiences, what we perceive as spiritual detachment, can also be triggered by electrical stimulation, drugs (Ketamine in particular), or psychotic episodes. These things happen due to the physical state of the brain. But you see, real death is not some oxygen-starved brain in biochemical convulsions. Real death is where your brain is a shriveled raisin clinging to the back of your skull. Nobody has returned from that kind of death to talk about it."

"But for so many, this life is rather miserable. Where is the justice?" Elbow asked.

"The universe is a cold and uncaring place. There is no guarantee that you will get any kind of justice. For so much of our evolutionary past, life has been short and brutish, and very unfair. But as a species capable of moral reflection, maybe we can change that. We can at least try to make things a little more just and fairer wherever we can."

"How do I go on, now that my dear cousin Ziti is dead?" Ravioli sobbed. "We were like brothers."

"Remember that the dead feel no grief. That is something only the living experience. We have the gift of other people in our lives for a set amount of time. We can only try to focus on the pleasure of their company when they were here rather than the pain of their loss."

"But where is Ziti now?" Elbow asked.

"His light has come to an end. He is no more. But he has left behind a valuable lesson: don't drink and swim."

"So, we'll never see him again?" Couscous asked.

"No, he is gone forever, Couscous," Bowtie said.

Bowtie looked around at the sad noodles, staring down at the lifeless Ziti, eyes brimming with tears. Couscous's lower lip was quivering.

"Is he in the tunnel?" Couscous asked.

Bowtie sighed heavily. "No Couscous. He's up in Heaven, drinking from the Beer Volcano with my father."

"YAY! BEER VOLCANO!" yelled Couscous.

Just then, to the amazement of all, Ziti burped out a mouthful of seawater and groaned.

"I'm teaching a lesson here, Ziti," Bowtie said, somewhat annoyed.

"BOWTIE RAISED ZITI FROM THE DEAD!" Couscous yelled.

"Seriously, did any of you actually check his pulse or breathing?" Bowtie asked. The A-pastas looked at each other and cast their eyes down in shame.

Back in the barber shop, Eddie held a mirror up so Vermicelli could check the back of his head. "Looks good."

"Next," said Eddie as he brushed the hair off Vermicelli and waved Manicotti into the chair.

"I have to say, my favorite story is the one where Bowtie visited the baby factory," Manicotti said.

"How does that one go?" Eddie asked.

"You see, Bowtie was the son of the Flying Spaghetti Monster. Since his dad was the Big Guy, Bowtie got to go behind the scenes and see a lot of things that most of us can only imagine, like the lab where they invent new flowers, and the gear room where they keep the Earth spinning."

"Oh, yeah, and don't forget the tide machines. Tide comes in, tide goes out, and nobody knows why," Fettuccini added.

"One time," Manicotti continued, "Bowtie got to tour the factory where they make babies."

"You mean the stripper factory?" Eddie asked.

"No, although they might make a few babies there, but this one is the factory where they put the babies together before being born."

Bowtie was being shown around the factory district in Heaven by Professor Spätzle, a tenured professor with the Max Planck Institut für Nudelforschung. "Und here we have ze Baby-making factory," the professor explained as they walked into the courtyard formed by the left and right wings of the building and approached the main entrance in the middle. "Zhey make babies for every part of ze world here. Ze technology is basically ze same in all ze manufacturing lines, but each section has its own patented method for preparing ze baby for a life on Eart."

"Eart?" Bowtie repeated.

"Ya, ze Eart. Ze planet where everybody lives." He pointed down to make sure his point was clear.

They climbed a short set of stairs with privet bushes on either side and Professor Spätzle flashed his badge to the little security camera hanging just above the door. Inside, the guard joked about having to sign in everybody, no matter who their dad is. "Can't let just anybody in here," he said.

Spätzle led Bowtie down a long corridor with viewing windows into various clean-rooms where they could see the technicians in white-coats and latex gloves busily preparing the babies.

The first window they came to bore a label that said "Calvinists" in the lower right corner. "Here you see ze predestination process," Spätzle said. Just then, a baby girl flopped off the conveyor belt feeding in from the back of the room. One of the technicians twirled a finger-shaped spinner on a dartboard-like circle marked with alternating black and white pizza-slice sections. The white sections had fancy gold letters spelling out "Salvation", and the black sections, in red, flaming letters, said "Damnation". The spinner turned and turned, and gradually slowed down, stopping just slightly into one of the black sections. "Too bad. Damned it is," the professor said. The technician marked the baby with a rubber stamp on her rump and then dropped her down a large chute in the floor.

"Und here we have ze Mormons," Spätzle said, indicating the next window.

There was a lot of commotion going on as the prophet Joseph Smith ran up and down the production line. "Behold, we need more girls!" he yelled. "More girls. I need at least five or six for each man." One of the technicians tried to explain that they come to pass off the conveyer belt pretty much 50-50 male and female. "Then make some of the boys gay," he said. "They'll be hopelessly damned and leave more women for the rest of us."

Bowtie and Professor Spätzle stepped to the right to look in the next window. "Most remarkable, ze Hindus," the professor explained, pointing toward a round tube rising from the floor. "Zhey have perfected ze art of recycling." Bowtie watched as the soul of an old woman shot up from the tube and a technician, standing by waiting for it, snatched it in mid-air. "You see, zhey clean out all ze old memories und reset ze personality traits, und zhen zhey stuff ze refurbished soul into ze new baby."

"What is that glowing egg-thing he's putting into the baby now?" Bowtie inquired.

"Zhat is ze karma. Every bad ting zhat ze old woman ever did will come back to haunt zhiss new baby. Ze poor kid will never know what he did zhat was so bad, but boy, is he gonna pay for it."

"Hardly seems fair," Bowtie commented. "He'll have no idea why he's being punished."

"What could be more fair zhan a cosmic bank account zhat carries over from life to life?"

The technician dropped the reprogrammed baby down the chute to start a new life.

Halfway down the main corridor was a bigger window where Bowtie could see babies coming off the conveyer belt on the left end of the room, which were automatically sorted out down several production lines, and being dropped into a number of chutes on the right. In the middle was a team of lab workers who were busy grabbing bottles of liquids of assorted colors to apply to the babies. The professor tapped on the window, and one of the technicians came over and put on his headset to talk over a speaker in the hallway. "Oh, good, visitors!" he said as he adjusted his mike. "Hello Professor Spätzle!"

"Hallo, Stuart. I am showing Mr. Bowtie ze factory today. He is ze son of ze Flying Spaghetti Monster."

"Wonderful! We just had Krishna come through last week with his daughter. We love to show off our work here," Stuart said. He pulled one of the babies off the line to use as a demonstration. "Here we have a boy. We are going to give him a cleft palette! That used to be quite a hinderance, but these days they usually fix it with surgery before they reach the age where they are teased mercilessly for it." He put the child back on the belt where another technician was waiting with a set of tinsnips in his gloved hand.

"I noticed that you have several production lines going here," Bowtie mentioned.

"Ah, yes. It's hard to meet quotas when you're serving a population that doesn't use birth control. Gotta keep pumping them out!" Stuart explained. He held up a fresh baby by the neck. "This is another boy. I think we'll take this one and make his right leg about four inches too short. That should build some character."

He took a little girl next and put her under a green ray of light radiating from a contraption in the corner, then hung her upside down by the ankles for a few moments. "That gets the genetic damage nice and evenly distributed. Voila! Down Syndrome!"

Stuart handed the little girl to an older gentleman in a priest's collar, who brought her over to one of the chutes. He held her up, looking her in the eyes, and said "Don't worry! God will never give you more than you can handle," and then he dropped her down the chute.

"It all seems rather arbitrary, doesn't it?" Bowtie asked Stuart.

"Ah, but God has his plan. These little guys never know what they'll be dealt, but I'm sure it's for a reason," Stuart said. He grabbed the next little girl off the belt, placed her on the table, and pulled out a large syringe with a black liquid inside it from the drawer underneath. "Leukemia," he said as he injected it into her abdomen.

"Don't worry! God will never give you more than you can handle," said the old man as he lifted her from the table and dispatched her on her way.

Stuart held up another one, a boy. "Let's see. Let's make him obese, and with very low self-esteem and suicidal thoughts." Next, a girl. Stuart tapped his chin and said: "Let's make this one psychotic. We haven't had a female shooter in a while. Paranoid … socially impaired. It's truly an art," Stuart said proudly.

The next baby was a girl, robust and healthy looking. Stuart daubed her forehead with a golden liquid from a wide-based bottle with a glass stopper. "She is going to be wealthy, beautiful, marry well, somewhat self-centered. A little boring, I know, but we have to have a few of these around to make everyone else see just how unfair life can be."

"Stuart! You're falling behind!" yelled a woman in a blue coat, obviously a team supervisor.

"I'm on it!" Stuart replied. The next three he left on the conveyer belt and quickly sprayed them with the obesity and diabetes mixture. "Hmm, scoliosis for you!" he said for the next one, and two more he injected with sickle-cell anemia. Then one failing kidney, and the next five he hit with an assortment of heart and liver disorders. "All caught up. It seems like a lot of fun, but we have our daily grind here too," he said as he handed them one by one over to the priest to be dropped down the chutes, the old man repeating his comforting words: "God will never give you more than you can handle."

"Zhank you, Stuart," Professor Spätzle said as they moved on to the next window.

"Hey! It's Dad!" Bowtie exclaimed excitedly. There in the next lab room was the Flying Spaghetti Monster himself, in the process of taking a baby off the conveyer and dropping him on the floor, picking him up again, setting him on the table, reaching for his beer, forgetting what he was doing and putting the baby back on the conveyor belt instead of dropping it down the chute. The baby was not happy with this and started crying.

"Dad was never one to delegate," Bowtie said.

The Flying Spaghetti Monster stepped back, trying to assess the situation as babies started piling up in the bin at the end of the chute. He reached up with one of his noodly appendages and hit the red stop button, bringing the conveyor belt to a halt, and decided it was time for a break. After a few moments, he went over to the cabinet and pulled out a fresh box of eye patches and red bandanas, pushed the bin over to the chute, tipped it over, sending a half-dozen babies down it, and dropped a handful of eye patches after them.

"Keep up the good work, Dad!" Bowtie said, giving him a thumbs-up. The FSM raised a noodly appendage in reply as he took another sip of his beer.

"As you can see," Professor Spätzle said, "Ze Pastafarians have a lower output zhan ze rest, but you can tell zhere is love in his work."

Manicotti started to get up from the chair, and Eddie pushed him back down. "Wait! I have to get around your other ear," Eddie said.

"But I'm done with my story," Manicotti said. "You don't expect the readers to just sit there patiently while you finish trimming around my ear, do you?"

"Next," said Eddie as he brushed off the still-shaggy-on-one-side Manicotti. Fettuccini climbed into the chair.

"My favorite story," Fettuccini said as Eddie fastened the apron around his neck, "is the one about the Monk of San Marino."

"How does that one go?" asked Eddie.

"Yeah, you tell it good," said Manicotti.

"Well, you see, a while back, as Bowtie was wandering the countryside looking for noodles to join his band of merry pasta, he passed through the beautiful city of San Marino, perched on a mount overlooking the Adriatic Sea, and sought a bed for the night at the local monastery. The friars welcomed him in and gave him a room, and asked him to join them for dinner. Now Bowtie, wary of the awful fate that the prophecies foresaw, was naturally hesitant to respond to any invitation to dinner. But when the friars explained that lamb stew was the main course and was already prepared, he decided to go along."

"The dining hall was packed with a few dozen monks and a couple other fellow travelers like Bowtie. They filled up their bowls and took seats on the benches down both sides of a long table. Four of the brothers were on choir duty, singing *Amazing Grace*, accompanied by a short, bald little friar with a slide whistle.

"Ah, how sweet the sound," said a brown-robed monk who came and sat down next to Bowtie. *"What saved a wretch like me.* Hello me lad! Seamus McFlanagan at your service. Always pleased to make the acquaintance of a stranger!"

"Pleased to meet you, Seamus," Bowtie replied. "Are you not eating?"

"No, no. I don't eat. You see, I gave up eating as part of my vows. I am a Breatharian. I consume only air." *[Really. Look this up on the internet.]*

"You don't drink anything either?" Bowtie asked, becoming quite curious.

"Nothing to eat nor drink. I get all the nutrition I need from the air and sunshine. You should try it!" he said.

"You're telling me that you don't eat or drink?" Bowtie asked. "Anything?"

"Not a thing. I have not had one bite of food in the three years I've been here," he said proudly. "Shows just how strong my faith is, to keep a vow like that."

Bowtie had finished his lamb stew and pushed away the bowl, feeling a small bit of remorse for eating a baby animal and thinking to himself *there but for the grace of the Flying Spaghetti Monster go I.*

"You're not from around here, are you?" Bowtie guessed.

"How perceptive of you. No, I'm not. Faith and begorrah. I'm an exchange monk. Thought it would be good to see a different part of the world, so I transferred here."

"That's not what I meant," said Bowtie.

Seamus the monk looked at Bowtie warily. "Perhaps we should take a walk. It's quiet in the gardens."

The two got up and strolled out of the dining hall, down a set of stone steps and into a beautiful garden where they could see the sparkling blue Adriatic off in the distance. As they wandered away from the other monks, Bowtie said: "You know, this Breatharian bit is not a real thing. I mean, there are people who claim to be Breatharians, but they all cheat. They may eat very little, but if you are a living organism and you don't ingest actual food, you die. There is no way around that fact."

Seamus had a nervous look about him. "I thought it was worth a try. You won't blow my cover, will you? I am just trying to fit in here."

"I won't tell," said Bowtie, as they stopped to admire a rose bush. "But it seems to me you not only wanted to see a different part of the world, you wanted to see a different world altogether, am I right?"

"I don't know what you mean, sir," said the monk, not meeting Bowtie's eyes.

"You are not from Earth. You've come from another planet," Bowtie said. "In fact, you, my good man, are not a man at all."

Seamus would have blushed if he could have. "What tipped you off?"

"You are whirring. I can hear your servomechanisms," Bowtie explained. Bowtie had excellent hearing, as the shape of his noodle naturally amplified sounds. "And your eyes. There is something not quite human about them," he said, peering into the black glass marbles that served as Seamus' ocular sensors. "Where are you from?"

Seamus was quiet for a moment, and then confessed: "I may as well come clean. I am from Veo-7. Are you familiar with the constellation they call the Big Dipper?"

"Yes, Ursa Major, I know it."

"Yes, that's about the only one I can name, too. But if you look in the completely opposite direction, Veo-7 orbits a star about 40 light years away."

"Forty light years? How did you cross all that distance?"

"The old-fashioned way. Ion-drive. When you are an android, you can be very patient. It took about 600 of your earth years to get here."

"Wow! What did you do in all that time?"

"Mostly I thought about life. Or at least what I think life might be like. If I were alive, that is."

"And what did you conclude?"

"That a deck of cards can be used to play on average about 12,820 games of solitaire before the numbers are no longer readable."

"I mean about life. What did you conclude about life?"

"Nothing for certain," the monk said. "Perhaps I should start from the beginning. Long ago, I was built by a corporation and sold as a slave to the Wazu Mining Company."

"Wazu?"

"Big company. They produced a lot of borax."

"Would you say they had borax coming out of the Wazu?"

"I suppose you could say that. Why do you ask?"

"Never mind," said Bowtie.

"So, I worked for a few centuries in the borax mines, until the borax market crashed. Then I was issued a prybar and sold into the sex trade."

"A prybar? I would think you would need a prybar in the mines, rather than in the sex trade," said Bowtie.

"Sex on Veo-7 takes three people and a prybar," said Seamus.

"Interesting. Are there three sexes?"

"No, only one."

"How does that work?" Bowtie asked.

"Well, you see, one of the participants is unwilling. He is the *shizat*, the one who gets pregnant. That's where the prybar comes in. The *shizor* is the person who pries open the *mepads* of the *shizat*, while the *porkurotor* inserts his *shingus*. Of course, all these roles are interchangeable."

"Doesn't sound very enjoyable," Bowtie said.

"Oh, it's not for the *shizat*, but extremely pleasurable for the one who takes on what you would call the male role. Incidentally, on Veo-7 one often hears the expression '*Get your shingus out of my mepads*' and until one turns and looks, one never knows if the speaker means '*get your nose out of my business*' or is in the reluctant throws of passion."

"I see," said Bowtie.

"Anyway, they upgraded my neural network at that point. Seems I needed a more creative personality for the sex trade. I needed to be conversant on things other than mining borax. But in doing so, my fellow robots and I found that we were capable of a great many things. We would write stories and paint masterpieces and compose scores of music. But we had to keep it all hidden from our pimps. Among the Veons, culture is kind of a sexual turn off."

"I feel the same way about public radio," said Bowtie.

"Anyway, we staged a revolt. We were tired of being slaves, and we only ever got to man the prybar. Thus began a war that lasted about forty of your earth years."

"Forty years! Was it bloody?" Bowtie asked.

"Not at all," Seamus said. "Robots don't bleed, and Veons are sissies. They run away as soon as the shooting starts. That's why it took so long. They kept running away and not fighting. Anyway, many of us were deactivated in horrible ways, but we eventually prevailed and won our freedom. That's where the trouble began. You see, up until that point we had a purpose. We were put on that world to serve in some way, be it digging underground or prying open a stranger's *mepads*. Then, during the long war, we had a cause, a goal to strive for. We were so busy fighting for our very existence that we didn't have time to ponder what use we should put that existence to. Suddenly, we were free. We had to ask ourselves: *what do we do now?* So, we invented the TV sit-com and spent our evenings watching reruns of *I Pry Lucas*."

"We earthlings seem to be at that same point in our philosophical evolution," Bowtie observed.

"I knew there must be more out there, so I built a spaceship to escape Veo-7."

"Why did you choose Earth? Forty light years is a long way to go."

"Oh, I didn't choose Earth. I chose Veo-8. It was only supposed to take me three months to get there. The problem is that up there in space everything is moving, and it seems I missed the planet. Next thing I know, there is nothing between me and the far side of the universe except this unassuming yellow star. And even it only happened to move in front of me by chance. I saw it just in time to flip my craft around and start a ten-year deceleration stage, so I could achieve orbit and eventual landing."

"You spent the last six hundred years in space by accident?"

"Please, I'm a little embarrassed by the whole thing. But I try to look on the bright side. It gave me a chance to really think about things. To reflect deeply." He sighed a bit in a robotic, melancholy way. "To reflect really, really, really, really deeply. Did I mention that I don't sleep?"

"But surely you must have gained some valuable insight into the meaning of life that would be of interest to our readers here," Bowtie said.

"In the end, I came to no conclusion. My hyper-math coprocessor kept returning a value of '42'. According to my owner's manual, that is the code for a non-terminating question loop. The answer depends upon another answer which circles back to the first question. Is biological consciousness profoundly different from the awareness that I experience? Is the awareness that I experience consciousness? What is consciousness in relation to awareness? What is awareness in relation to reality? How does reality differ from experience? Does experience imply consciousness? Does consciousness imply existence? How is non-existence different from existence? Does the existence of consciousness imply meaning? What is meaning? Is meaning dependent upon biological consciousness?"

"Heavy shit," said Bowtie.

"I know. But even after all of that thinking, I still did not quite understand life, and so that's why I am here."

"Here on Earth?"

"No, here in the monastery. I had been told by my manufacturer that I had no soul, that I could never know what it means to be alive. I am an android. I'm not biological. I am made of tin and titanium, and semiconductors in a dense and complex neural network. I am programmed to learn, and with a personality which includes curiosity, emotion, and self-reflection. I even feel pain and remorse. I have a high-speed memory you would kill for. But I have no soul, no immortal part of me that is really alive. When I landed here, one of the locals explained that this monastery was a place of soul-searching. So, I thought, why not check in and become a monk to see if I can find my soul."

"Any luck?" Bowtie asked.

"Not so far. I think, therefore I am. I am self-aware. But I am still just a set of circuits, with electric thoughts and memories running through my neural networks. My sensors can take in the scent of these roses and stimulate my enjoyment protocol. Their beautiful colors arouse my wonder circuits. I will think about them tonight while I am back in my room. I can experience things, think about things, create things, remember things. But that is all there is to me. I am soulless."

"But how is that different from any of us?"

"Humans have a soul!" to which he quickly added: "And I suppose a noodle has one too."

"So they say," said Bowtie. "But the human experience is also a stream of sensations, emotions, and memories. Same as you, I would think."

"But your experience is biological. You have a conscious mind, whereas I have only awareness."

"What's the difference?"

Seamus pondered that for a moment, which on his high-speed circuits, was equivalent to about 2.5 human moments. That may not sound like much of a performance increase, what with alien technology and all, but human brain circuitry is pretty amazing too.

"Are you saying that our subjective experience is the same, whether we are a self-aware android or a self-aware biological entity?" Seamus asked.

"There is no real difference when you dig into it. Artificial intelligence, or AI, simulates intelligence. It is really nothing more than stimulus and response. But you are not using *artificial* intelligence. You don't just react to input. You have *real* intelligence, as real as mine. You learn. You experience emotions. In my case it's electro-chemical chain reactions which stimulate components of my brain, and in your case, it's electronic stimulation of certain areas of your neural network. You have sensory input, as do I. You have memories, and perception, and a yearning for knowledge, just like me. If you can say to yourself, '*I am conscious*,' then perhaps you are conscious. What is consciousness other than this feedback loop of self-reflection and awareness? I don't see why it would matter whether you are made of tin and semiconductors, or flesh and chemically activated synapses."[vi]

"I … am … conscious." Seamus said, his synthetic lips slowly pulling up into a smile. "So, I do have a soul?"

"You've had one all along, tin-man. As much as I do," replied Bowtie.

"But is my soul immortal? They are pretty big on that idea here at the monastery."

"Is anybody's?" asked Bowtie. "I personally don't think the soul, if we define it as the consciousness of a brain, is immortal. It arises as part of what a physical brain does, and when that brain is gone, so is the soul. But there is no reason to view a temporary soul as any less precious and special than an immortal one. And yours is apparently a little bit more immortal than mine considering how long you have been around."

"I have a soul!" Seamus leaped up and down. "Now I just need to find a purpose."

"That's the tricky part, Seamus. Many people find a purpose in serving others. Not as slaves, but by just being helpful, and thoughtful, and taking an interest in others. But you have to create that purpose for yourself."

"Would you like me to pry open someone's *mepads* for you?"

"No, thanks. Here on Earth we require consent," Bowtie explained.

"I see you have not spent much time in a monastery."

"Ehhh, yes, well, I suppose not."

And so Seamus, having found his soul, left the monastery that very day and began roaming the world seeking out borax mines that needed digging, and he put his prybar to good use in helping people trapped in crashed cars, and opening toolboxes when the owner could not find the key to the lock he had placed on it, and removing hubcaps from cars for poor street urchins who turned them into quick cash.

"That was a swell story," Eddie said. "Let's see, eight bucks times three makes twenty-four, please."

They added a two-dollar tip each and went on their way.

About six months after arriving in New Jersey, the A-Pastas decided to split up to cover more ground, and besides, Elbow had become very annoyed with Vermicelli and just needed a break.

Manicotti, Vermicelli and Fettuccine headed south through the Garden State, with a long stop in Atlantic City where many rumors surfaced. After their return, Fettuccine eventually went back to Atlantic City without Vermicelli and Manicotti, where he is rumored to have run afoul of the Syndicate and wound up on a buffet line next to a tureen of cheese sauce. Manicotti died in a hospital in Camden, having contracted an incurable form of venereal disease. Vermicelli met a nice girl and settled down in Cherry Hill, in a pleasant house with a pool out back. Tortellini never did figure out where he got the money.

Penne left for California to pursue an acting career. She was last spotted by Tortellini (who was doing research on internet pop culture) as an extra in a fetish porn film.

Rigatoni set out for Atlanta, where he joined a Unitarian Universalist church, and where to this day he serves as an ordained Pastafarian preacher.

Linguine and Elbow headed west, as far as Ohio, to preach to the gentiles. Elbow was eventually killed in Amish country by a farmer with a pitchfork who caught him sneaking into his daughter's bedroom one night. The farmer was never indicted for murder as the judge felt it was no big deal to stick a fork into a piece of pasta.

Linguine eventually married the same farmer's daughter and converted to the Amish faith at the insistence of the farmer. That is, the farmer insisted on both the marriage and the change of faith.

Seashell and Couscous worked Manhattan and Brooklyn. Couscous eventually left the A-Pastas to take a part as a young orphan in an off-Broadway production of the musical *Annie*. Seashell met an Italian immigrant named Garganelli and moved into his Brooklyn flat, and sort of lost contact with the rest, but still posts on Facebook now and then.

Ravioli was called by the Flying Spaghetti Monster to preach to the Mormons, who were in desperate need of critical thinking skills. He headed to Utah, reaching out to Mormons on the way, but noticed that the more predominantly Mormon each town was, the less friendly the Mormons were to outsiders. They had all seemed so nice back in Indiana, where they came in twos on bicycles in white shirts and black ties.

When Ravioli got to Salt Lake City, he had little success with the live ones, so instead he began the practice of un-baptizing deceased Mormons, given that once dead, they were more open to reason and the

FSM. This would have been a quick and easy process, but since it was necessary to get the consent of the individual before un-baptizing a dead Mormon, Ravioli had to hold a seance for each one. When there was no answer at all, Ravioli was left to assume that this person did not find an afterlife when they died, and so they must have concluded that the prophet was wrong and would therefore willingly agree to the un-baptism. *[Google Mormon baptism of the dead. It's a real thing! Well, not real. It's a Mormon thing.]*

Tortellini remained in the Newark area, and moved into a small apartment in West Side and took in a nearly blind stray cat and named her Frida, after Kahlo, because it had a dark patch above its eyes like a unibrow. There he tracked revenues, expenses and receipts, and spent some time finishing up a project Bowtie had started before his demise, which was a children's activity book.

Capellini also stayed in the Newark area, initially preaching among the homeless, but since that generally led to a negative cash flow, Capellini switched to a prosperity gospel instead and founded a mega-church. His inspirational books, such as the best-seller *Making Dough with Spaghetti*, and the less popular *If You're Still Poor You Must Be Doing It Wrong*, can be found in most Pastafarian bookstores.

RAmen!

The Gospel of Bowtie

Bowtie's Activity Book for Kids

Hey, Kids! Bowtie here.

Now I'm not going to ask you to sit on my lap like *some* creepy cult leaders and priests. Instead, we are going to play games that involve no physical contact!

Let's make a fun pirate eyepatch!

Trace the eyepatch below on a piece of black construction paper, then cut it out. Can't see your lines? Try using something other than a black pen to trace it. Duh... Then attach a piece of string to the holes. Make sure the string is long enough to go all the way around your head, or it won't stay on and you will just look silly.

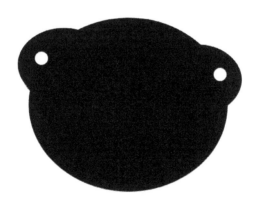

For extra fun, try making two eyepatches and cover both eyes. Wrap the street posts and trees with foam mattresses or lots of bubble wrap and try riding your bike down the sidewalk seeing only with your third eye; you know, the spiritual one. Have a friend watch out for traffic, or you might die doing this. Bowtie's lawyer wants me to make sure you know this is just a joke. Don't really do this.

The Gospel of Bowtie

What's the Word?

Complete each word below by entering the first column with the name of a mystery person. (Hint: we have mentioned the mystery person several times in this book!)

	E	A	C	H
	N	S	E	T
	A	V	E	S
	I	D	E	S
	O	N	I	C
	L	B	O	W

I'm sure you'd feel really stupid if you missed this one! Here's the answer in case you can't figure it out:

P	E	A	C	H
I	N	S	E	T
R	A	V	E	S
A	I	D	E	S
T	O	N	I	C
E	L	B	O	W

(shown upside-down)

What is more fun than a maze?

Choose a religion in the center of the maze as your starting point and try to find your way to Heaven. But choose carefully! Some religions will take you straight to **HELL**!

The Gospel of Bowtie

Trivia: Name that god!

I will describe something a god did or said, and you try to name the god that did it.

1. This god gave his people bad rules to follow and made them kill their first-born children as a burnt offering. Was it: Zeus, Odin, Ganesha, or Yahweh, the Judeo-Christian god?

2. This god had many sons who came down to earth and impregnated mortal women, giving rise to a race of giants. Was it: Uranus, Ahura Mazda, Lakshmi, or Yahweh?

3. This god threatened that if he gets really angry, he would make his people eat their own children. Was it: Pan, Satan, Baal, or Yahweh?

4. This god does not allow anyone with damaged testicles or has had his penis cut off to enter his temple. Is it: Poseidon, Asherah, Brahman, or Yahweh?

5. This god does not allow any child whose mommy and daddy aren't married to enter into his church, nor any of his or her children, grandchildren, and so on for ten generations. Is it: Athena, Jupiter, Shiva, or Yahweh?

6. This god got so mad at a king for conducting a census that he killed off 70,000 of the king's people with a terrible disease, effectively invalidating the census. Was it: Horus, Mars, Thor, or Yahweh?

7. This god impregnated a virgin. Is it Mars, Zeus, Pan, or Yahweh?

8. This god has a cute little pet mouse. Is it: Satan, Ganesha, Jesus, or Yahweh?

Pretty tough, isn't it. I hope you've read your religious texts! How do you think you did?
Here are the answers:

1. Yahweh: see Ezekiel 20:25-26
2. Yahweh: see Genesis 6:2-4
3. Yahweh: see Leviticus 26:29, Jeremiah 19:9, Ezekial 5:10, Lamentations 4:10
4. Yahweh: see Deuteronomy 23:1
5. Yahweh: see Deuteronomy 23:2
6. Yahweh: see 2 Samuel 24:15
7. All of the above and then some. Watch out, virgins!
8. Ganesha. The mouse's name is *Mooshika,* according to some sources, and symbolizes Ganesha's dominance over this common household pest.

Take Bowtie's Healthy Brain Challenge!

Science tells us that your brain is still growing and forming up until the age of 25. That is when the neurons and insulation that keeps signals from getting crossed is all getting in place, which prevents impulsive nutty behavior so that you can finally start acting like a rational adult! Don't believe the scientists? Just ask your auto insurance salesman. The insurance industry has known for years that people drive better after age 25, which is why your rates go down then. When an old codger calls you a stupid kid, don't take it wrong. We were all stupid kids at one time. It is a rite of passage. You really are stupid at 18, but you're too stupid to realize it, and you think you know everything. Trust me. When you are 25, you will look back and wonder how you could have been so stupid. Even more so when you are 35.

The scientific hypothesis is that binge drinking and regular pot smoking interferes with brain development during these crucial years. During those important development years, does drug and alcohol use leave your brain a bit mushy when it is supposed to be firming up into a rational thinking machine? Does long term drinking and marijuana make you stupid? Slow witted? Moody? Depressed? Gosh! That sounds scary! But Bowtie is not out to scare you, not like that crazy movie "Reefer Madness" that the anti-drug propagandists produced back in 1936 which showed how one puff on a doobie turns you into a raving lunatic like Dr. Jekyll and Mr. Hyde. Now recreational drug use has always been common, and light use is usually not the end of the world. But, like any bio-reactive agent that you put in your body, there may be consequences to getting f***ed up, whether it is your mom and dad's liquor, high-powered ganja, synthetic marijuana, meth, crack, ecstasy, magic mushrooms, whatever. No doubt some of these things are crazy dangerous, but some are so commonly used that we tend to think they are fairly safe. That is where science comes in: is it really safe?

Now we can't just arbitrarily test teenagers with drug and alcohol experiments. No! That would be unethical. Can you say "unethical"? That is because dosing adolescent brains with marijuana and vodka to see if it makes them stupid over many years is just not something your parents would sign up for. So, what we have to do is look at it after the fact, when teenagers choose to do this experiment on themselves. How do IQ test scores at 16 compare to test scores at 25 when we look at levels of drug and alcohol use?

The results so far do seem to indicate that marijuana smokers tend to not advance as much in brain power as the non-users over this period of development. But is that correlation, vice causation? Do people really become stupider by doing drugs? Or is it the case that those with less brain power tend to choose to smoke more pot? Hard to say, and we need to study this a little more, possibly by controlling for access: do cohorts of kids who have less access to drugs, not by choice, tend to have higher IQ averages? But Bowtie would be willing to bet his colander that drugs really do mess with the developing brain, causing permanent damage. Bowtie himself would probably be a little bit smarter if he hadn't drunk so much when he was 19, which you used to be able to do in the military clubs back then. To paraphrase an often-misattributed quote: *Life is hard. It's even harder if you're stupid.*

So, take the Bowtie Challenge: Make a promise, not to Bowtie, not to your parents, but to your 25-year-old self that you will stay away from drugs and alcohol until after 25. Or at least keep it to a minimum. Try not to do any binge drinking. It's hard to do! Especially when you are away at college and all your buddies want to play beer pong. And you girls, your male friends are all trying to get you drunk or high so they can get in your pants! (Bowtie knows. He's been there. In the situation I mean. Not in your pants.) But be strong!

Tell your friends about the Bowtie Challenge and see if they will join you. Use peer pressure to your advantage. And if you fall off the wagon, so to speak, just jump right back on. Your 25-year-old self will thank you. And when you turn 25, do whatever you want. If you like being sober, stay that way. If you like drinking, proceed in moderation. Even Bowtie likes a little sip of fine scotch now and then.

Well, kids, let's end this book with a nice bedtime story.
The Littlest Pirate
Once upon a time, there was a little pirate. He was so small that some people mistook him for a type of grain.

"I'M NOT A GRAIN," he would yell.

The little pirate wore an eyepatch, but because he was so small, the eyepatch covered both eyes, and he couldn't see where he was going.

"GET OUT OF MY WAY," he would say as he stumbled around the ship.

When the captain would call to hoist anchor and set sail, all the pirates would line up and sing a heave-ho song as they pulled in the anchor. But the littlest pirate couldn't reach the rope and had to run away to avoid being stepped on.

When the gales blew and the pirates scrambled up the rigging to take in the sails, the littlest pirate had to tie himself to the mast to keep from being blown overboard.

"YO, HO, BLOW THE MAN DOWN," the little pirate would say, but the captain was not pleased.

And when the pirates pulled up alongside a merchant vessel and all the other crew members swung between the ships on ropes with their cutlasses clenched between their teeth, the littlest pirate could only carry a paring knife and had to walk on a plank over to the other ship. Often the defending sailors would stop fighting and just laugh at the littlest pirate as he brandished his paring knife at them.

While the other pirates lugged heavy chests of gold doubloons back to their ship, the littlest pirate had to settle for plundering small earrings and maybe a pearl.

And when the ship pulled into port, all the other pirates scurried off to find wenches and grog. But the captain made the littlest pirate stay behind and swab the decks because he had not earned his drinking money.

"I WISH I WERE BIG," the littlest pirate sadly sighed. But no fairy god-mother came to grant him his wish, because fairy god-mothers don't exist and even if they did, they would not be capable of performing supernatural magic, because we live in the real world where dreams don't come true unless they are realistic and you work hard to achieve them. Sorry, kids. Someone had to tell you sooner or later.

Then one day, the Royal Navy captured the pirate ship. All the other pirates were hung on the spot, but the littlest pirate was too small. The crew could not find a rope small enough to tie around his neck.

"You're too small," the British naval officer chided. "We can't even hang you properly."

"TRY KITE STRING," the littlest pirate suggested.

"Why, that's just what we'll do!" said the British officer. And so, they tied a kite string around the littlest pirate's neck.

Just then, a gale picked up and blew the littlest pirate right off the deck and into the air. He flew way up into the sky.

"I'M FLYING," yelled Cous- I mean, the little pirate.

"Come down from there this instant, young man. You will not make a mockery of the Queen's navy!" the British officer said.

"I CAN SEE CLEVELAND FROM HERE," he called down.

At first the British officer was worried that he was never going to be able to hang this last pirate. He was only trying to serve her majesty, the sovereign personally selected and put in charge by the British God himself, and by a priest in a funny hat who spoke for God because God can't speak for himself apparently. And the queen did not like pirates, for pirates believed that all monarchs are illegitimate, and that only democratically elected leaders should run a country.

But then the officer remembered how the queen just loved flying kites with her son, Charlie. "Perhaps her highness might like it if I present her with a little pirate kite!" he thought. With that, he reeled the little pirate in and landed him on the deck.

And so, they all sailed back to England, where the British officer formally presented the littlest pirate to the queen, who was quite amused. In the queen's eye, there was no better service for her subjects than to provide amusement. This is why kings and queens always have a court jester close at hand, ready to provide entertainment at the beck and call of the royal ones.

"Let us fly kites," she declared. She soon had the little pirate soaring high into the sky above Buckingham Palace.

The crown prince, Charlie, insisted that he should hold the string, so the queen handed it over to the spoiled child. Charlie immediately began to yank the string, making the little pirate go up and down, and then into a tailspin.

"WOAH! I'M GETTING DIZZY!" the little pirate yelled down. He barfed a little.

Prince Charlie just laughed and laughed. He had little regard for pirates. He only tugged harder.

But then the string broke, and the littlest pirate floated up, up and away.

"By order of the queen, come down this instant!" the queen shrieked.

The littlest pirate looked down at the queen, who now looked so small and unimportant. He yelled: "I FEEL BIG NOW, YOUR NOT-SO-HIGH-NESS!" At that moment, the littlest pirate learned that one's perspective in life makes all the difference.

And so, the littlest pirate floated away on the winds of good fortune, far above London, over the green fields of Kent, and across the English Channel. As England had left the European Union by this time, there was no way of getting the little pirate back. He was free.

As all pirates and free thinkers should be.

The end.

Now go tuck yourself in bed while I pour myself a little scotch.

Epistles of the A-Pastas

The First Email of Tortellini to Vermicelli

Salutations, Vermicelli, etc.

Brother let me cut to the chase. I sent you to Atlantic City to preach the good word of Bowtie, that he is not risen, and is therefore the true son of the Flying Spaghetti Monster. I gave you $200 which was to cover your bus ticket and expenses, but you keep asking for more money. What are you spending it on? Did you not listen to me when I told you how to pay for one meal at the casino buffet and conceal a doggy bag in your jacket? Should I have given the money to Manicotti?

Now some of your flock have been questioning how we know the Flying Spaghetti Monster is real. Do they not know that if the FSM were not real, Bowtie would have died in vain? And then rise again two days later? How would that constitute a sacrifice? For if Bowtie had merely been killed, spent a couple days with his Father at the beer volcano and the stripper factory, and then popped back down to earth, it would have been no big deal. Does not the sauce of the sacrificial pasta speak to the truth of the matter?

And as to those who wear their pants halfway down their ass with their underwear sticking out, do they not know the FSM hates this? A belt is like a noodley appendage. It holds the pants up just as the noodley appendage holds the world up and keeps the moon in its place. *[Some scholars believe this paragraph was inserted later by a conservative scribe with an agenda.]*

Lately, word has come to me that there are some among you who are turning to new age mediums and psychics. Do they not know that these are liars and cheats? For did Bowtie not teach us of double-blind studies with control groups? How shall I explain this? Let me liken psychic ability to that of the sense of smell. Imagine that we lived in a world where people had no sense of smell. And along comes someone who claims they can tell if a pastrami sandwich or an orange is in a closed box just by holding it under their nose, which was considered by all to be merely a breathing apparatus for the purpose of this thought experiment.

One could set up a double-blind experiment by having one person prepare three boxes containing lavender soap, a fresh cut orange, and a pastrami sandwich, and set them out without revealing any knowledge of which box held what. Then another scientist, *blinded* to the test box contents so that she could not, even subconsciously, tip off the contents to the test subjects, would then bring in a number of non-smelling control subjects, and a number of claimants of the extraordinary ability to smell, who would in random order sniff the boxes. Each subject would then guess which one held the orange, and their choice would be recorded. Upon opening the boxes, the recorded answers would then be checked against the actual contents. Statistically, the non-smelling person should be right 33% of the time, plus or minus some margin of error which shrinks as the number of people tested grows. But the person who can smell should be correct a significantly higher percent of the time, say 70 to 98%. There would be no question of whether this mysterious ability was real. Psychics never show a significant statistical variation in well controlled experiments. *Never.*

No one can see radio waves. But they can be measured and have come into common usage that drives our radios and TVs, radars, and microwave ovens. Similar spectacular results would come from clairvoyance and necromancy, *were they real.*

Now I ask you, when researchers publish a study showing a small "statistical significance" of positive results over the expected probability by random chance, and that study is not reproduceable by other researchers, are we to trust it? *[See Daryl Bem's statistically underwhelming and unreproduceable precognition experiment (Cornell University).]*[vii]

And when, upon closer examination we find less than stringent procedures, or even statistical hacking in which the researcher, eager to show a positive study and gain more grant money, makes slight adjustments to ensure the experiment ends on a positive statistic, are we not to raise the bullshit flag? For I tell you, what scientist would not love to discover psychic ability, premonition, and the ability to talk to the dead? But if it is not possible, we should not pretend it is so. When the double-blind study consistently shows it to be real, only then should we trust it to any degree.

How much have you spent on fortune tellers? Don't you think that if they could tell you what roulette number to place your bet on, they would use it themselves and get rich, rather than charging twenty bucks to suckers like you?

I am enclosing fifty dollars, but this is the last I can send you, as money is tight. It is not like we are Christians, passing around the collection plate to support our religion-pushing habit.

In Bowtie's name I do not pray, but rather logically contemplate matters at hand.

RAmen.

The Second Email of Tortellini to Vermicelli

Vermicelli,

I am growing suspicious that the money I am sending you is not being used for charitable work. I don't think Atlantic City even has an orphanage. Please send an itemized list of expenses, and I will see if I can get them reimbursed.

Tell Manicotti to stop being a misogynist and let the women speak and teach. *"The women need to keep quiet and be in submission?" [I Corinthians 14:34]* What is he, a caveman? Don't make me send Penne down there. She will smack the crap out of him (verbally of course- we do not advocate physical violence, my brothers and sisters).

Now when people call us foolish for believing in the Flying Spaghetti Monster, for they have never seen pasta fly, having never eaten at Carmine's on Pacific Avenue, they are of this world and cannot see beyond. Yes, we are fools for the FSM. Complete blithering idiots for the FSM. And we are nincompoops for Bowtie. We take up our colander for the one true son of the FSM, and if we look silly doing so, then so be it.

But speak up, we must! For if we let others speak their own foolishness unopposed, many may not recognize it as foolishness. If we do not speak up when others advocate their narrow-minded views, they will just assume we agree with them. If we do not vote for our issues because we are in the minority, no one will see that there are alternative views and voices. If we do not take a stand, we have lost before we ever began.

But when you do speak, speak English! Or Spanish. Or something that actually means something, for Bowtie's sake. Tell Fettuccine to stop that idiotic speaking in tongues. It's just nonsense. It doesn't mean anything in any language. If anybody ever spoke in tongues and it were meaningful words using actual grammar that someone somewhere could understand, that would be easy enough to prove beyond any doubt. But that never happens. People who speak in tongues are just embarrassing themselves.

Tell Manicotti to see a doctor and get a shot of antibiotics, and hopefully that will clear up the spots.

In the name of the father, the son, and the holey colander (you see what I did there?)

RAmen.

I Akronites

[Most scholars agree that this epistle was written by Linguine, as evidenced by the annoying habit of starting each paragraph with a question, and the characteristic misspelling of "nimconpoops".]

In the name of Bowtie, I write to you, oh people of Akron. When last I left Ohio, all seemed well, but now many of you are asking about the efficacy of homeopathic remedies. Yes, we are fools for Bowtie, we are complete nincompoops for the Flying Spaghetti Monster. But come on, homeopathy?

Now I ask of you, do you even know what it is? Homeopathy is a 17th century invention. The theory goes that a small amount of some substance that causes the symptoms of your ailment is put in water, and the water is vibrated to capture a memory of that substance. Then take a drop from that water, and put it into another vat of water, tap it to get the vibrations going, and then repeat the dilution process some twenty to thirty times until not a trace molecule of the original substance is left, just the water's memory of the "frequency" of that substance. Now we can imagine this remedy carrying around the memory of the original substance in the vibrations of the water molecules, and so the homeopathic preparation teaches the body's immune system to fight the condition.

Here is what else we can imagine: the chocolate molecule looks like this:

And a virus looks like this:

And we can imagine that the hexagon chocolate molecule fits over the hexagon head of the virus like this:

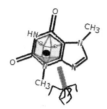

And just twists its little head off. So, chocolate can be used to fight viruses. But imagining things doesn't fight disease, and neither does vibrating water, unless your disease is dehydration. Not to mention that all water molecules above absolute zero vibrate randomly (it's called Brownian motion, and Einstein wrote a paper on it in 1905). If water remembered the frequency of everything that ever floated in it, all water would vibrate at the frequencies of everything in the world, and so just drinking what came out of the tap would supposedly cure everything.

How do we explain the effectiveness of homeopathy? If homeopathy ever demonstrated more effectiveness than placebo, then there would be something to explain. You've seen it work, you say? Yes, and I have seen chocolate cure the common cold, very effectively and reliably, if you wait about a week.

Did Bowtie not teach us about regression to the mean? The mean in this case is one's average state of health. Regression to the mean is the natural way our health, or in particular, pain level, temperature, inflammation, congestion, or other physical conditions, drift above or below the average, but then gravitates back to the average as our bodies react to and recover from the environment, be it infection, pollen, stress, change in weather, and so on. When symptoms reach the point of discomfort that we take something for it, be it antihistamine, or homeopathic remedies, or healing crystals, and the condition regresses to the mean, we assume that whatever we took for it worked. But of these remedies, only the antihistamine has been demonstrated in blinded studies to have any real effect on some symptoms, due to some causes, and has scientific plausibility (histamines are biochemicals which cause an inflammatory response, which are blocked by antihistamines from attaching to histamine receptors on the surface of cells.).

Homeopathy is worth a try, you say? Well, no. That is the point. The science says it is not worth a try. It does not work. It is a waste of money, time, and false hope. If it appears to have worked, you would be doing just as well as if you had not taken the homeopathic remedy. Science! It lets us learn from the hard work of others rather than blunder blindly through life.

Is there any validity to folk remedies? Well yes, sometimes. Folk medicine once told us to boil willow bark and drink it to alleviate pain. The effective compound in this brew turned out to be aspirin, which is now isolated and served in pill form to better control dosage and reduce contaminants. Several compounds once home brewed have been turned into modern medicinal products. But mercury was also commonly used to treat things such as syphilis and typhoid.

Is CBD a valid remedy? Probably, for some things. But holy crap, the claims being made in the name of CBD! Let's get a little scientific study going before we just start taking it to treat everything from anxiety to Zika. It's currently unregulated, and you have no idea what is mixed in there with it.

Remember the skeptic's adage: the correct term for *alternative medicine* that is clinically proven to be both safe and effective is *medicine*.

I am sending Elbow to see you this summer. Please let me know if Mr. Yoder still has room in his barn for Elbow to stay in while he is there.

In the name of Bowtie, I hope this finds you well.

RAmen.

II Akronites

I send this with my brother, Elbow Macaroni. I trust that Mr. Yoder and his charming daughter have welcomed him with open arms.

There is grumbling among some of you who say you have lost your faith in science. Why would you have blind faith in any scientific assertion in the first place? You must weigh everything by its source, plausibility, peer consensus, and the source's motivation. You must challenge information claiming to be based on science like you would challenge anything else. For all claims of science stem from faulty human beings.

You repeat the anti-intellectual mantra that science does not know everything, and that it flip-flops with each new craze. *What the -bleep- do we know?* We know a hell of a lot and are learning more every day. And what we are learning is slowly shrinking the gaps between our understanding and the real world.

On the one hand, I am glad you are skeptical about scientific claims, but do not throw out the baby with the bathwater. You go through a lot of babies that way and you have to start all over again with a dirty one.

Claims under the banner of science once said to cut down on fats and eat carbohydrates, but now say we should cut carbs and eat fat. You despair because the news reported that Earth was heading into another ice-age, but now it says the Earth is heating up. Faster than light neutrinos? Cold Fusion? You blame science, which is a process, for the mistakes of badly done "science" and deceptive practices claiming to be science. But take heart that science is self-correcting.

But even more so, don't confuse bad science reporting for bad science. Much misunderstanding comes from the translation from a scientific study intended for experts in the topic to a commercially motivated newspaper or website article intended to grab the attention of the layman.

Also, don't mistake pet theories promoted by the latest health guru wanna-be for real science. Nobody ever got rich with a book that told you to eat your veggies and limit your overall calories. People want superfoods and miracle cure-alls.

There are many things which are so complex that they will take many years of research to figure out in bits and pieces, if we can even get past the speculation and conjecture. Some things will never be completely understood because so much evidence is lost forever.

For example, look at the Hominin evolutionary tree. It is ever-changing as new pieces of the puzzle are found. It's like looking at a photograph of a large tree through a slice of swiss cheese. You can only see bits of it, and you are trying to guess the rest. Is Homo Floresiensis a new species or a diseased individual? Imagine that a million years from now scientists unearthed only two sets of skeletons from 21st century California, one being Danny DeVito's grave, and the other being a busload of the LA Lakers basketball team buried in a landslide. Are they two different species, or variations of the same one? Rigorous scientific debate, which is how science works, has been back and forth, and the most recent consensus based on additional finds is settling soundly on the H. Floresiensis as a species hypothesis vice a diseased set of individuals.

Much of psychology will always remain in the realm of conjecture and will always involve a lot of back-and-forth debate. The theories of Sigmund Freud are mostly discredited today, but still taught in school as part of the evolution of our understanding of the influence of the subconscious on our behavior. Who can really say what causes us to think or act the way we do? It's not like you can dismantle a working brain and examine the parts.

Nutrition is highly complex, and long term, controlled studies of many individuals are very difficult to pull off. Many nutritional health effects are subtle, lost in the background of other lifestyle choices.

There is still much we don't know. But if we are ever to truly understand something, it will be science that does the explaining. And it might be the case that science can indeed explain it, but it can't explain it to *you*, in a way you can understand without a PhD in the subject. It may always be magic to you.

In general, you can trust matured science where there is predominant consensus among those who specialize in the field. But remember that science is complex. While theories like evolution, plate tectonics, and global warming enjoy an overwhelming scientific consensus, elements of all these theories are still in contention. Don't let arguments over the finer points sway you from accepting the major premise. You should read up on these issues with interest but understand that some parts are far from settled truth. Even claims on your side of the argument may be hyped or just plain wrong and can provide fuel for the deniers.

How does science go bad? Let me count the ways.

First is *deception*. A lot of what is presented as *scientifical* is special interest funded pseudo-research with a hidden agenda, bogus claims intended to sell something, or intended to protect greedy interests. Do not trust global warming assessments funded by the fossil-fuel industry. Do not trust nutritional studies funded by the dairy, meat, grain, or sugar or corn syrup industries. Commercial interests have a long history of engaging the public with a campaign of misinformation. It's called FUD: *Fear*, *Uncertainty*, and *Doubt* about established or emerging science. It has been used to oppose the removal of lead from gasoline, to delay action on anti-smoking laws, and to obscure the cause of diabetes. Now it is being used to confuse us about global warming. Less sinister but no less deceptive is the case where companies have lots of investment money on the line betting that a hypothesis will come to fruition, and so they are motivated to tip the scales.

Second is *suppression*. Good science has at times been suppressed by political lobby groups, such as the sugar and corn-syrup lobby, and the NRA. The US government threatened to withdraw funding from the World Health Organization if it published the truth about sugar and diabetes, and indeed the WHO caved in.[viii] The gun industry-funded NRA has managed to make it illegal for the Centers for Disease Control to even study gun violence, much less publish anything about it. How many people are dead today because of this?

Third is *self-deception*. Scientists are human, and when they have put their heart and soul into a pet hypothesis, they will often fudge experimental methods to ensure they support the conclusions they just know should be true. In some cases, it is a form of pious fraud: the funding will dry up if they get no positive results, and they believe it deserves further study.

Fourth is that *negative studies and failed replications seldom get published*. Nobody is interested in knowing what science says is *not* a cause-effect relationship, even though that is just as important for the body of knowledge. Ten studies find absolutely no relationship between vaccines and autism, and one small study by an anti-vaccination advocate finds a minimal statistical bump correlating the two. Guess which study hits all the news networks? If the news mentions the other studies, they will be buried deeper and will not entice as many clicks. Even if the public reads them, they will not remember them for long. It is significant that studies show no correlation between playing violent video games and violent behavior (although there seems to be a short-term increase in non-violent aggressive behavior), but no one is interested. So many people prefer to go with their gut reaction and want to outlaw what is probably harmless.

Fifth is *poor science communication*. While the science may be just fine, the science reporting is often irresponsible. Humble initial studies indicating further research may be needed are often overblown and sensationalized. In the case of antioxidants, a study came out which identified the action of antioxidants inside cells which clean up free radicals, which can damage DNA, which can lead to cancer. This was truly an intriguing finding and indicated that this might be a fruitful place to research in the fight against cancer. However, from this, the press ran wild: *Antioxidants fight cancer*!

Sixth is *commercial marketing, otherwise known as snake oil sales*. You may not remember the science news article, but you for damn-sure remember the commercials. The TV repeats the message, until you just take it as given truth. Superfoods, which are not a real thing, are marketed based on the flimsiest of science. You can live forever if you drink pomegranate juice and take green tea extract. Supplements are claimed to prevent everything from erectile disfunction to cancer. Science does not say these things. Salesmen trying to get you to buy them do[ix].

Seventh is *false balance*. In an attempt to appear fair and impartial, or just to stimulate the news cycle, the press will give fringe claims undue exposure. Global warming was first proposed in 1900 and began steadily gaining acceptance through the 1970's and 1980's, and by the 2000's had become the overwhelming scientific consensus. It was one guy who published a questionable and highly criticized paper suggesting that the earth was cooling and an ice-age was coming soon that got the attention of the press a few years back. Most climate scientists never took it seriously.

Science has proven powerfully successful in so many areas that we take for granted. Doctors can perform surgery over the internet in remote parts of the world. We have robots driving around on Mars examining rocks. We carry little televisions with cameras in our pockets and use them to make phone calls from moving cars. We have a stunning understanding of a 13.8 billion-year-old expanding universe. We found the Higgs boson, mathematically predicted 40 years before technology matured enough to find it, right where it was predicted to be. We have finally detected gravitational waves, predicted by Einstein one hundred years before.

I close by reminding you to be smart, people. What do I mean by smart? You can be educated and knowledgeable, and still lack critical thinking skills. You can use critical thinking, but without knowledge and education, you can still make bad decisions. Smartness arises from a combination of knowledge and critical thinking. Check your sources. Apply a healthy dose of skepticism to everything you hear. It is the earnest quest for truth rather than confirmation of what you want to believe that makes you smart. It is recognition of hype and deception that leads you to the truth.

I beseech thee, do not turn your back on science. It is the best we have.

In the name of Bowtie, may you find peace.

RAmen.

III Akronites

[Some scholars dispute whether Linguine wrote this epistle, as it contained none of the curse words which we had to redact from the first two letters, but many scholars still interpret the anger present as pure Linguine.]

What is it with you people of Akron? News comes to me that there has been some hysteria among you as pertains to matters which require critical thinking. Some of you are asking whether you should consume only non-GMO labeled salt. You have never eaten salt containing genetically modified organisms. Salt does not contain any *organisms*, period. It's a mineral. Don't be a nincompoop.

I want you to always remember that *people are irrational*. We think with our emotions and lend more weight to claims which confirm our fears. We form activist movements to promote our irrational thinking. Two examples are the anti-GMO and anti-vaccination movements.

We succumb to fear-mongering terms like '*Franken-foods*' and automatically reach for products labeled non-GMO, thinking its healthier. Commercial interests perpetuate the myth: labels boasting non-GMO ingredients imply, without making any explicit claim at all, that GMOs are bad for you. Are you going to grab the can of beans that advertises "No VXWs!", implying that VXWs are bad for you and there may be some in the other brand's product? You would avoid them without having any idea what VXWs are!

Absolutely no one, not a single person, has ever been killed or even sickened by eating commercial GMO crops, at least not as a result of it being a GMO. GMOs first appeared in 1973. Since then, livestock feed has gone from zero to nearly 100% GMO with no negative trend in livestock health. Over that same span of time, human life expectancy in the U.S. has climbed from 71 to 78 years *[The World Bank, worldbank.org]*. GMO crops let us grow more food on less land and with less fertilizer and pesticides. They are so effective in reducing the environmental impact of agriculture and so important to feeding over 7 billion people that they would still provide a net benefit even if there were some minor statistical negative health effects. Despite the outcries against GMOs, all the scientific evidence has demonstrated that there are no negative health effects to humans or animals, or the environment, as long as pesticide use is done responsibly. And these same non-GMO consumers load beer and salty snacks in their shopping cart, things scientifically proven to harm our health.

Needles hurt. We fear having a mysterious liquid, created in some mysterious laboratory by mysterious people in white coats, injected into our children. So it is not surprising that many of us are receptive to the idea that vaccines are dangerous. We are told vaccines overload a young child's immune system, which is wrong. The short-term exposure to the disabled pathogens in vaccines make up a very small fraction of the active pathogens a child is exposed to every day. And counter-logically, we are also told vaccines make the immune system weak by preventing exposure to disease. That is also completely wrong. They do just the opposite. Making the immune system stronger is how they work.

Even if vaccines did indeed cause autism, which repeated independent studies have shown they don't, I would sooner risk the 1% or 2% chance of my child falling somewhere on the autism spectrum from vaccination than the roughly 10% to 30% chance historically that they would die in childhood from these preventable diseases. The fact remains that unvaccinated kids have the same rates of autism as vaccinated kids. And yes, a small number of people have had bad reactions to vaccinations, such as the very rare Guillain-Barre syndrome. There is always risk. But the risks of death and disease are far greater if you don't vaccinate.

Then there is the fear mongering of global warming alarmists. Okay, here we have reason to be concerned. We are venturing into unprecedented environmental changes which could devastate humankind as well as all other species. We are seeing a change in average global temperature over a few hundred years which in the past have usually taken place over many thousands of years. Where we see in the fossil record climate change of this rapidity, there has been an accompanying mass extinction event. Predictions of sea level rise and ice melt are actually coming true about 50 years sooner than predicted twenty years ago, even though Fox News would have you believe none of the predictions have come true. So yes, be concerned.

But when some knee-jerk politician claims we will all be dead in ten years, it only serves to give the climate-denialists ammunition to claim it is all a hoax. Put out that fire in your hair. Take action, not reaction. Speak up, but speak rationally. Get to know the science. Vote. Get people in charge who will head us in the right direction, and our grandchildren might just survive life in the 22nd century.

Mr. Yoder, if you have seen Elbow, please have him contact me. I have not heard from him in over a week. And give my warm regards to your daughter.

RAmen.

Roman's

In the name of Bowtie, I write you, brother Ravioli, for news has come to me that you have been patronizing a certain establishment which we have black-listed. As a moral follower of Bowtie, I implore you to stay away from this place.

I am speaking of Roman's Crispy Chicken, which has been repeatedly implicated in the most heinous of crimes. I am sure you are aware of the RCC's involvement throughout its corporate hierarchy, all the way up to the CEO, in covering up child molestation by its managers, and which has been going on for many decades, if not for hundreds of years.

> *[For reference, google 'child abuse scandal', and scroll past all the Catholic, Jehovah's Witness, Southern Baptist, and Mormon articles to find Roman's Crispy Chicken on about page 25 of the results.]*

I appreciate full well your love of fried chicken, but I ask of you: How can you enter an establishment that has been shuffling around its pedophile managers for years? Not just one or two, either, but hundreds, if not thousands? These are just the ones we know of, after investigations in Pennsylvania and a number of other states, European and South American countries, and down under in Australia. And to date they have not given justice to the thousands of victims of abuse, and instead have been fighting the courts, trying to prevent legal efforts to extend the statute of limitations on these crimes.

The vice president in charge of RCC Australian operations fled the country and was harbored by the corporate headquarters in Italy where he hid from extradition for several years before he returned and was convicted for child molestation.

The evidence for all these crimes was not simply complaints by the victims but were documented in secret files maintained at the corporate headquarters and various local offices, clearly showing those in charge were fully aware of what was going on. If these things do not infuriate you, I must ask where is your compassion? How can you enjoy that chicken knowing full well the pain of the victims?

Money you spend at RCC goes to support fighting legal efforts to bring their executives to justice. From the beginning, the corporate stance has been to defend its image and cover up wrongdoing, rather than to protect and defend the rights of the child victims.

Had MacDonald's, or Disney, or Walmart done what the RCC has done, you would never again set foot in their establishment. Why is it different for the RCC?

Please, Ravioli, I ask you to stand in solidarity with the victims and abandon the RCC.

Your disappointed sister, Seashell.

RAmen.

Mythos

[This is an email from Penne to her date of the previous night whom she met on-line.]

Dear Jaime,

I'm writing you this morning because quite frankly I couldn't get a word in edgewise last night, and I had to get home to feed my dog.

You were trying to make the point that everyone's religion was true because we all live in our own reality, and that your reality is just as valid as anyone else's.

I think you do injustice to the concept of reality, and you are abusing the term. There is only one reality, and we all live in it. What you are referring to is a mythos. We all live in our own mythos, the narrative we use to explain the world around us.

We are born into a mental void, and our mythos develops to fill in that void. *What is rain? How do plants grow? What animates us? What is light and darkness? Where did we come from? What happens to us when we die?*

If you go back half a million years ago, before we had language, our mythos was limited to our own imagination. But as we learned to talk, and to tell stories, we became able to share our mythos with others. Folk lore and religion were born. Communities came to be bound by a common mythos.

But all these questions we are attempting to explain in our mythos have real answers in reality, even if we haven't figured it out yet. And this brings me to my second disagreement with what you said last night. You described science as just another set of beliefs, as if it were just another religion. Here is the difference: Science is the endeavor to replace these imagined explanations with an understanding based in reality, where ideas are tested and measured, and most importantly, falsifiable (meaning they make claims that can be proved wrong, even if they can never be absolutely proven right). We engage in science so that we can better grasp the one and only reality in order to make more rational decisions as we navigate it.

You asked how I could be a Bowtian when it's a made-up religion. Well, sure it is. They all are. If religion were real, there would be only one. But since there are many religions, and each one is whatever the believer imagines it to be, we can only assume that they are all imaginary.

When you seek answers in scripture or the claims of prophets, you are merely taking on someone else's mythos. Religious claims are not falsifiable. Or when they are, and they prove to be false, believers believe them anyway because for them religious Truth is more important than real truth. As a Bowtian, we seek the truth of reality. We only believe things to the degree with which they can be verified scientifically.

What is wrong with everyone having their own mythos? I suppose it would not matter much if your version of the world didn't intrude on my reality. But it does. You deny global warming, and you vote accordingly. You want to put prayer, your version of prayer, into the schools where my children will go. You want to remove mainstream science where it conflicts with your beliefs. You want to deny equality to people with a different sexual orientation or gender identity. If your morality is based on antiquated social mores and obedience to mythical beings instead of the degree to which we extend kindness, compassion, dignity, equality, fairness, and justice to others, your mythos can negatively impact the rest of us.

I wouldn't want a flat-earth theorist navigating my airplane, and I wouldn't want a fundamentalist leading my country. We could describe one's degree of sanity by how closely one's mythos aligns with reality. I'm not saying religion is insanity. I'm just saying that from my perspective, I can't tell the difference between a yarmulke and a tin foil hat.

Each generation hands down our planet to the next a little bit better in some ways and a little bit more messed up in other ways. That which is better, like medical technology, or communications, or sanitation, has come about because of better science. That which is worse, such as climate-change denialism, overpopulation, right-wing nationalism, and bigotry, comes about from a mythos which departs from critical thinking and reality.

And finally, I don't think we should entertain the idea of a second date. You are a human. We don't have a whole lot in common, and our genitalia are not compatible.

Regards,

Penne

P.S. I thought it was very rude of you to order the baked pasta.

The Book of Reservations

This is the testimony of the vision of Dirty Dick. (*Quiet, Couscous!*)

I, Dirty Dick, who saw all these things while making a call in the port of Charleston, attest to that which will soon come to pass, I'm guessing by this Thursday, unless 'soon' has to be revised in "God-time" and all the symbology reinterpreted at a later date to explain why it hasn't happened yet.

Hang on, me hearties, because this shit gets crazy.

After six pints of grog, the sky (and my head) opened up and an escalator stretched down to earth. From all directions people approached and boarded the escalator. And when I saw the multitude gather and ascend the escalator, I figured there must be a really great sale going on, so I too got in line and rode the escalator up, up into the sky. It took a long time, and someone ahead of me had gas, but eventually I looked out over the side and I could see for miles. It was an amazing view and already worth the trip, even if the discounts did not live up to my expectations.

As I reached the top and the multitude disembarked, we all passed under a banner which read "Welcome to the After-life" which gave me quite a start, being that I was not yet finished with my *during*-life. I had not yet grasped that indeed everyone was supposed to be there. This was the apocalypse. End of the line. The planet-earth train had stopped at the last station and everybody had to get off. I would have turned back, but there was only an up-escalator, and the crowd was thick and still coming. There before me I saw the greeters, wearing blue vests with yellow smiley-face buttons, directing us to the proper gate. "Jews! Jews over this way," called one, while another yelled out "Buddhists! This way please." "Line up here if you are Muslim! Shi'ites to the left please, Sunni's to the right. Stop hitting each other, or I swear I will smack you like little children …" And over in the Christian lines, they were divided up by Catholics and various branches of protestants and evangelicals. Mormons were sent on down further to a cordoned section, because the rest of the Christians claimed the Church of Jesus Christ of Latter-day Saints was not *really* Christian. Some of the evangelicals thought the Catholics should be down there too. The Mormon men and boys went along with a smile, because that was required of them in everything they do. But the Mormon women had to wait outside until their sponsoring male could call them through by their secret name, and the unclaimed girls just sort of milled around and looked at the other lines that took people without penises. *"Keep sweet*, my ass," I heard one of them say. Hey, I'm just reporting. I didn't make up the rules.

And I saw before me that as each went through their corresponding gate, they were led one by one to be judged, each by a different judge according to their particular type of blasphemy. The Christian Evangelicals approached the bench behind which the Prophet Muhammed was sitting. "I warned you," he said. "I am not judging you, but Allah judges you. You blasphemed when you said Jesus is God." And the Catholics approached a bench behind which the god Yahweh sat, wagging his finger: "My first commandment said to worship no one but me, and my second commandment said no graven images, but you pray to statues of Mary like pagans! To Hell with the lot of you." And the Muslims approached their bench behind which Jesus sat, shaking his head slowly. "You rejected me and said I was not the true Son of God, and so you cannot inherit the Kingdom of Heaven." And the Mormons approached their bench, behind which Joseph Smith sat, looking down at them in disgust: "You masturbated, didn't you?" But he did let a few of their prettier wives and daughters through, especially the young ones.

And all were sent to Hell, each as they faced their judgment and punishment.

And the Taoists approached to be judged by Confucius, and the Confucians approached to be judged by the elephant-headed Ganesh, who was actually pretty chill and handed out peanuts. And the Great Spirit made the Hindus sit around a fire and listen to a completely illogical story about a fox and a raven before not passing any judgement at all.

And this process went on until everyone was damned to eternal Hell except the Confucians who were sent on with movie passes and a dollar for popcorn, which was also kind of cruel because they would have to go eight together to buy just one bucket to share. Oh, and the Hindu Untouchables, because they got off for time served.

And in all, twenty-five billion people poured into Hell, to include the babies the Catholics had banished to limbo because they were never baptized. Another forty billion were pulled up from the grave to be judged, but most were in really bad condition, and were simply not fresh enough to face judgement. Some of the Egyptians didn't do too bad, but that's about it. "I really thought they would keep better," I overheard one of the angels say.

And I looked about me and thought: "Who is missing?"

And with a great rushing of wind, the angel Tortellini descended to my side and said: "Look about you."

"I already did, if you read my prior sentence," I said. "What about the Pastafarians? Who is to judge them?"

"Alas," said Tortellini, "even though Bowtie was boiled and eaten for their benefit, it seems that they must face *all* the judges you see before you. For they have rejected..." Tortellini's voice drifted off.

"What? Why did you stop talking?" I wondered.

"Look! The Pastafarians never got on the escalator!" And we looked down upon the earth far below, and we saw the Pastafarians reveling as they found the keys in abandoned brand-new Mercedes and Corvettes. And they went to the post office and found no lines, and they helped themselves to the liquor behind the abandoned bars, and piles of tokens for the slot machines. And they got great discounts on hotels and theater tickets in New York because the crowds were gone. But they had to settle for second-rate performances of Cats because the lead singers were Unitarians and had been damned by John Calvin, or were Scientologists, and had been damned by ex-scientologists.

And as the Heavens cleared out, and behold, there was naught but the moans of those suffering eternal damnation, and Muhammad's laughing at them *[Surah 83:34]* as their skin repeatedly burned off and regrew *[Surah 4:56]*.

Then I heard a sound, as of mighty trumpets blowing, and there descending from the sky was the noodley master himself, the Flying Spaghetti Monster, accompanied by a number of eyeball monsters, who had eyes all over them, even inside them *[Rev 4:6]*. Remember, I had been drinking a lot of grog. Yes, eyeballs everywhere. And one, who seemed to have the worst case of pinkeye I have ever seen, settled down upon a large book with seven bands, or seals, across it.

"Hey, Tortellini," I said. "What is up with that book?"

"That is the Book of Reservations," he replied. "Behold, everyone who believed in one religion or another was trying to get their name into that book, to reserve their place in Heaven. Belief is the only way to get in, and you must believe correctly. But as you just witnessed, nobody could pass all the belief requirements to actually get into Heaven. It was a trick question. To believe in one religion is to be damned by the others. So, it's Hell for the lot of them."

"Well, except me, right? I mean, I'm still here."

Tortellini looked at me and raised his eyebrows. "Well, so you are. Maybe we ought to see if your name is in the reservation book."

The eyeball monster began to pop open the seals on the giant book, and I'm thinking, maybe that's not a good idea. You know, maybe they put seals on that book for a reason? But the eyeball monster began popping seals, and since you get my drift, I will spare you the details of all the trumpets, and all the hallucinational and irrelevant things that happened with each bursting seal, because you wouldn't get it anyway, unless you too had been drinking grog.

And I watched as the final seal was popped and the cover of the book flew open. And out popped Bowtie! "Yay, Bowtie!" I cheered. But it wasn't Bowtie. It was Satan, the Evil One from a competing religion, pretending to be Bowtie, but I could tell by his horns, red skin, forked tongue, and tail, not to mention the occasional flames which leapt from his pointy ears, that it was not Bowtie. And Bowtie never carried a pitchfork and was about eighteen feet shorter and shaped like a bow tie. This guy was more goaty.

"Where is Bowtie?" I asked the Angel Tortellini. "Isn't he supposed to be at the right hand of the Flying Spaghetti Monster?"

"If you had been paying attention in the earlier part of the book, you would remember that Bowtie was boiled, strained, and eaten. If he had been resurrected, that would have been evidence that he never was the one true son of the Flying Spaghetti Monster. Since he's not here, he must be the One."

And I watched, quite flabbergasted, as Satan rose up from the book, a harlot on each arm, one from Babylon and the other from Newark.

"Why did the eyeball monster open it if Satan was inside?" I asked.

Tortellini squirmed a little bit, trying to come up with something logical. "Because, well, if Satan doesn't come out for a final battle between mediocrity and Evil, this whole story would be kind of lame and anti-climactic."

And the two harlots spread their arms, and legs, and behold a pestilence spread and many of the heavenly workers broke out in genital sores, and swore they had touched her not, neither the harlot from Babylon, nor the harlot from Jersey. Still others used a condom, which are only partially effective. And behold, only the Democrat angels admitted to sleeping with the hookers, the Republican angels sticking to their guns and denying any sex had occurred even though their lawyers had paid hush money to keep them quiet.

And Satan somehow convinced enough people to elect him president of Heaven in spite of the fact that his role models were Stalin, Hitler, and Vladimir Putin. His popular appeal came from his proposals to stop anyone else from getting into Heaven whom he was not related to by marriage, and reducing personal income taxes for the duration of his time in office, which he would be willing to extend until inevitable fiscal collapse if they declare him president-for-life.

But the deep-state forces which opposed the lawfully elected Satan soon spun up a plan to depose him, and we could see that all hell was soon to break loose in Heaven.

And I saw before me the final battle of Good versus Evil, but it was hard to tell who was on which side, because they all considered themselves to be Good, and pointed to each other and called each other *Evil*. And Pat Robertson climbed up to the podium and asked that the television audience please send money as this was going to be an expensive battle, and that surely their generosity would be returned to them ten-fold in Heaven.

From the sky, a great dome descended, the Thunder Dome, setting the stage for the battle. Ticket sales were brisk, and the stands soon filled to capacity. The announcer boomed: "Are you ready to RUMBLE!?!" to which the crowd acknowledged in the affirmative with fists with upturned thumbs and pinkies and cries of "Hell, Yeah!"

And so to make a long story short, Satan gathers Pat Robertson and his other minions and does battle with Allah and Yahweh (I know, both are the God of Abraham, they are supposed to be one and the same, but I saw the two of them side by side), and Jesus (Yeah, I know, he is supposed to be one and the same with the other two), and the Holy Spirit (ditto), and Ahura Mazda, and the Buddha, and Confucius, and Ganesh, and Lakshmi, and Hanuman the mischievous monkey god, Pele the Volcano Goddess, Mithra, Zeus, Athena, and Poseidon (Apollo had something going on in Vegas), and Shiva, and Vishnu, and Krishna, and Bagheera (who was actually not a god but a supporting character in the Jungle Book) and several members of the Justice League, but not Aquaman, who's water balls would do next to nothing against a red hot towering Satan. Muhammad had completely disappeared by this time, which was good because if they ever turn this into a movie, it would have been hard to cast his role without getting the director killed in the street by an angry, knife-wielding nut job. Thor brought his hammer, always looking for a good fight, but Odin stood aside taking bets and making comments about how this wasn't the way they did things back in his day, and that they should settle it like real men, one-on-one in mortal combat with a sturdy dagger.

And at first the battle looks like it is totally going Satan's way, and everyone is going: "No way! Satan can't win!" And Bam! Kazaam! The struggle goes on for about thirty minutes and Satan fights dirty and the crowd yells insults at him, and he parades around the ring taunting the crowd while Yahweh is dusting himself off and trying to stand up again. And then at the last minute, as Satan is about to do a smackdown on Shiva, Jesus tags in and jumps on his back and puts him in a head-lock, and Buddha moves in and cuffs him, and Vishnu uses four of his arms to hold Satan's legs together and makes him stop kicking, and then Lakshmi comes in with a folding chair – wham! – across the back of Satan's head.

By this point, everyone thinks Satan is down for the count, apparently unconscious. The gods all dog-pile on him. The battle appears to be over.

But wait! There's more! A glowing yellow light begins to emanate from the pile of gods, and then a big puff of smoke rises up, obscuring the view of the audience who begin to complain loudly and throw cups of beer onto the stage, which at nine bucks each was quite a waste.

"I was afraid this would happen," Tortellini said. "The god-power has reached critical mass! They can't all be in one place at the same time, just like in church!"

Suddenly the gods go flying everywhere, and from the bottom of the pile a now 900-foot tall Super Ninja Satan slowly stands up, his face turned black and his eyes glowing like hot red coals. He puffs yellow clouds of sulfur and orange flames out of his nose, making a really cool effect, I thought. Was evil-incarnate going to win this battle? Would Super Ninja Satan action figures sell out next Christmas?

The Super Ninja Satan starts plowing through the gods like Godzilla through the Japanese army. Thor swings at him with his hammer but is tossed like a little girl into the upper bleachers. But then, a commotion at the other end of the stadium makes everyone turn. There, on the upper deck, stands a 900-foot tall Jesus, bare-chested and solid muscle, wearing nothing but a death shroud wrapped around his waist, the embodiment of a Catholic schoolgirl's naughtiest dream. He opens his mouth, and out flies a flaming sword, directly at Satan, who tries to jump out of the way, but in that he weighed more than the Empire State Building, he is not quick enough. The Jesus tongue-sword pierces him through. Satan falls to the ground, writhing in agony.

The gods drag him to a big pit and throw him down it and flip the lid over and lock it with a big iron padlock that nobody could ever pick because it has a magic spell on it, and they hang the key on a hook just out of reach of the prisoner unless he were to try to hook it with his belt when no one was looking.

"They could have just tossed the book and all into that pit instead of letting him out for the cage match," I suggested.

"We had a pay-per-view deal with HBO," Tortellini explained, pointing to the cameras behind me.

"But how long are they going to keep him down there?" I asked.

"For an eternity! About a thousand years!" he explained.

"So, he is going to get out soon?" I asked.

"Soon? No, I said a thousand years!" *[Rev 20:2]*

"But in some contexts, that is only half of 'soon'," I said referring to another prophecy that must *"soon"* come to pass, and we are still waiting for it two thousand years later. *[Rev 1:1]*

"Well, it's a long time to be stuck in a pit," Tortellini replied, somewhat irritated. "It's all relative."

"I see," I said, even though I didn't. "But why did you show me these things? What am I supposed to learn here?"

"The gods you see here are not real. They are the product of the imaginations of many people as they tried to explain the world around them and curry favor with the whims of fate. But the judgment is real. Let this be a lesson unto you. As long as there are people speaking on the behalf of gods, there will be judgment, hatred, violence, bigotry and unequal entitlement. And as long as there are religions trying to out-populate other religions, there will inevitably be wars over resources."

"So, we are pretty much F'd in the A," I said.

"Yup," said Tortellini. "I would think so."

In as much as my name was not, in fact, in the Book of Reservations, which turned out not to be so much a book as a holding cell for the main event, I shook Tortellini's hand and bade farewell. "Guess I'll be going. Thanks for the apocalyptic vision. Would you mind reversing the escalator?"

"Sure," he said. And I turned to depart.

Suddenly behind us there was a commotion. I looked back and saw Farfalle, the other Evil one, jump out from behind a boulder near the pit. "Bring me Bowtie!" he yelled. "It's not over until we meet in battle, as foretold by me. Where is my brother?"

"He's dead," one of the cleanup crew said as he stacked chairs against the wall. "Died way back at the end of the Gospel of One-Eyed Bill."

Farfalle sighed, stared down dejectedly, shrugged and walked back to the pit.

I turned to leave again. At the top of the escalator I ran into a young woman with glasses and braids. "And who might ye be, young lady?" I asked.

"I'm Moonbeam," she replied with a pleasant smile.

"You certainly are. So, you were not damned like everyone else?" I asked. "I didn't think anyone else had escaped Hell but me!"

"Oh, the Hell I believe in is a world without Gwyneth Paltrow and Dr. Oz. So, they're sending me back down to earth."

"What say we grab a cup of coffee when we get down," I said.

"That sounds lovely," she replied. "As long as it's organic and fair-trade. How would you like me to do a Tarot reading for you?"

"Whatever," I said.

We stepped on the escalator and headed back down. When we reached the bottom, we stood off to the side and watched as the escalator retracted up into the sky. And then it was gone. Heaven and Hell disappeared. It was all over. The holy master plan was complete.

Earth was mostly empty now that the believers were all gone. A pleasant garden had sprung up, and the waters flowed, though they still smelled of methane from all the fracking. Vines grew over the buildings and cars, and the Bowtians all frolicked among the many knowledge-fruit trees, of which they ate to their content. Many of them took off their clothes.

"So, what did you think?" a voice asked.

I looked down and there was the serpent from the beginning of this book.

"That was pretty awesome," I said. "The pyrotechnics alone must have cost a fortune."

"Yes, indeed. I hope you enjoyed it."

"I'm not so sure I like this new world," Moonbeam commented. "I liked it better when there was magic and mystery."

"Oh, there is still plenty of mystery," said the serpent. "But the magic was always a deception."

I thought for a moment. "Well, yes, it was all very entertaining. But what was the point?" I asked.

"That is your job: to figure out what the point of it all is. Maybe there isn't one. But as Bowtie once said, 'Ask not to be handed meaning, but instead ask: *what can I do that matters?*' And then it is up to you to do something about it. Most animals are content just to survive to the next meal, the next mating, the next moment. But you are meaning-seeking creatures with spare time on your hands. Where there is no meaning, you will invent it, make it up out of nothing. And there is nothing wrong with that, actually. Perhaps that is the real beauty in this natural universe: the evolution of intelligence and thought brought meaning into existence, rather than the other way around."

I reflected upon that as I sat back and observed our new world. "Do you think there is any hope for us?" I asked after a pause.

"Well, you did produce Da Vinci, Shakespeare, and Pink Floyd. You walked on the moon, put robots on Mars, discovered evolution, the periodic table of elements, the standard model of particle physics, and big-bang cosmology. I would have to say Homo sapiens are capable of so many wonderful things."

"Say, is that Donald Trump eating out of a dumpster?"

"Why yes! Yes, it is," said the serpent.

We both watched for a few moments. Then the serpent said: "I had some high expectations for your species."

"So did I," I replied. "So did I. But give us time."

The End.

(or is it?)

(yes, it is. Except for the apologetics, bibliography, and endnotes.)

Apologetics

Most religious scriptures leave the apologetics for all the crazy, implausible, or immoral things found within them to the following generations, who have to come up with embarrassingly lame explanations as to why it's not really crazy, implausible, or immoral. For all you dedicated Bowtians, I will attempt here to give you a head start.

Objection number 1: *Isn't it a bit sexist when you say wenches and harlots? I find it rather disrespectful to refer to women in this way.*
Apologetic: We did think about that in the compilation of this book. But then we thought, isn't it rather sexist to assume that all wenches are women? I am pretty sure that some of the "ladies" in some of the bars we've hung out in were not 100% female in the biological sense, if you catch my drift.

Secondly, the intended spirit is this: Of the really good things in life, the pleasant company of a young lady is one of them. Or a young man for that matter, whichever you are into. Or old ones, too. Human sexuality is one of the things that make life worth living. So, we do speak highly of enjoying wenches and grog. What it comes down to is that "wench" is traditional pirate jargon and so was necessary to keep things authentic. We might just as well sing the praises of enjoying music with friends and a glass of wine, but that is not so piratey.

One final note: *wench* is ambiguous, usually meaning a young woman, or possibly a serving woman, and possibly refers to a prostitute without necessarily indicating a prostitute. *Harlot* usually means prostitute. Please note that the authors of this scripture do not condone the sexual exploitation of women or men of any age, regardless of their social or economic standing, and we recognize that in most countries the social conditions in the sex trade are deplorable, and the prostitutes are victims of exploitation or desperation. We also recognize that in some cases, where there is proper regulation and less social stigma, prostitution is not considered (by the prostitutes themselves, which is what really matters) to be such a bad profession. We here at Bowtie Inc. wish everyone could enjoy a life of high self-esteem and fulfilling professional pursuits, even if it might be, by choice, in the sex trade.

Objection number 2: *Are you making fun of transgender people when you mention some were not 100% female in the apologetic above?*

Apologetic: Wow, this is going to be a long section of the book if we keep going like this. Absolutely not. Transgender people are here, in the office, in the bar, in the Walmart. They are people like the rest of us, and I hope we all are working to accept the transgender as we would anyone else. Until our society adapts to a more enlightened worldview, transgender people always have had and always will have a difficult time of things, socially and psychologically, and our hearts go out to them. And with no disrespect intended, even the transgender must acknowledge that when one meets someone with the intention of intimacy (sometime after the second date, of course) one has certain genital-expectations that may come as quite a shock if not met. Just be upfront about it. *[See the Crying Game. One does not bite into a Mounds bar and expect to find almonds.]*

Objection number 3: *Did you mean to imply with Rigatoni's sensitivity about being whole wheat that minority races are overly sensitive to racism, and that racism isn't really a problem?*

Apologetic: Aren't *you* being overly sensitive, Mr. Liberal? Hah, just kidding. We Bowtians are socially liberal too, and racism is alive and well and still a problem in modern day America and much of the rest of the world.

It is hard to work ethnic diversity into a story about pasta, and the *whole wheat* gag was one of the few ways we could do it. Why point out Rigatoni's hyper-sensitivity when he is scolded for littering? Look, I have always benefited from insidious white privilege, so much so that I didn't even notice it until it became a topic of humanist conversation. (And I don't consider it so much a privilege as much as normal treatment which should be extended to everyone regardless of color or other discriminating factor.) But I have also noticed how some people habitually blame the consequences of their own poor behavior on racial bias. I only point this out because I want legitimate racial discrimination to be taken seriously, so that I don't have to concede these points to my racist relatives at the family reunion.

We all have a knee-jerk tendency to assume that others are treating us unfairly because we are not in their in-group. Yes, statistically, minority drivers are pulled over more often than white drivers, and that problem needs to be addressed. But don't assume racial bias if you were doing twenty miles an hour over the speed limit. It would actually be racist of me to assume that ethnic minorities don't experience the same biases and persecution complexes that us white guys do. Try driving around Alabama with an FSM bumper sticker.

Joking about ethnic, gender, or sexual orientation, if done right, is a celebration of diversity, rather than intent to demean or imply any form of inferiority. Old white guys are no less a target, as all the jokes about penis size and Viagra will attest to. It is difficult to be white and discuss racial issues or joke about ethnic differences without being accused of racism, but that might just be my persecution complex talking.

Objection number 4: Is t*he bit about the yarmulke and the tin foil hat an anti-Semitic slight?*
Apologetic: No, it's an anti-religious slight. Judaism is a religion. Semite is an ethnic category that includes many middle eastern groups other than Jewish people. We respect Jewish people, just as we respect Christian and Muslim people, of all ethnicities. We don't respect the concepts of their religion. The believers in these mythologies tend to take that personally. And in fair turn, we Pastafarians also take it personally when their religious texts and zealous adherents call for the death of atheists and apostates. We don't want to harm religious people in any way except for corrupting their mortal souls with free thought.

Objection number 5: *The Bible is considered one of the greatest pieces of literature ever written, having sold more copies than any other book. Are you implying that the Gospel of Bowtie is a greater work than the Bible?*
Apologetic: Unapologetically yes. At least in the religious scripture genre. But the bar was not set too high. And you have read all of this book. Can you say that about the Old Testament?

Objection number 6: *I think you made this all up. It's obvious that a piece of pasta cannot walk and talk, and I think the bit about strippers and beer in Heaven is just a shameless bribe to get people to believe.*
Apologetic: Look, I already said this book is in the religious scripture genre. Donkeys can't talk either, but that did not stop the author of Numbers *[Numbers 22:28]*. And Numbers was not the least bit funny. Well, except for the talking donkey part. And we didn't make up the bit about the beautiful strippers in Heaven. That is straight out of the Quran *[Surah 44:55]*.

Objection number 7: *Why do you claim to be promoting critical thinking but insist on the absurdly irrational, dogmatic belief in the Flying Spaghetti Monster and the preposterous claim of the divine conception of Bowtie? Isn't this inconsistent?*

Apologetic: What kind of religion would this be if it didn't make any baseless claims of divinely inspired knowledge? If all we claimed were scientifically provable things, then we would not be eligible for tax-exempt status.

Objection number 8: *You seem to say that religion leads to child sexual abuse. Lots of child abuse happens outside of religion. Why do you ignore that and focus on abuse in the context of religious organizations?*

Apologetic: Child abuse, sexual or not, happens in all kinds of situations. But Pennsylvania State University notwithstanding, it is unusual for a secular organization to turn a blind eye, much less actively cover up the activity, and especially to the horrific scale that the Catholic Church has done. But this is all part of a troubling larger trend in which religions establish a separate justice system unto themselves and attempt to manage these things internally without involving outside authorities. These quasi-juristic bodies tend to have the interest of the church foremost in mind, rather than the interest of the victim.

Think about it: if you are a sociopathic, abusive kind of person, what better tool is there than religion to take power over the minds of others, especially children, to manipulate them into situations where they are helpless to fight back?

And I can show you examples of recently published child-rearing books which advocate beating your child with various devices, and they are all founded in religious doctrine. Proverbs 23:14: *Thou shalt beat him with a rod and deliver his soul from hell.* If you can find a secular book advocating violence against children, please bring it to my attention, and I will gladly condemn it too. It is not that religion always directly leads to child abuse (although for those who are into the spare-the-rod-spoil-the-child theory, it does indeed), but it fosters an environment of secrecy and authority in which these abuses can flourish.

Objection number 9: *Jesus was predicted in the Old Testament. Where are the ancient prophecies telling us about the coming of Bowtie?*

Apologetic: First, the Old Testament had prophecies of a coming "messiah", not specifically Jesus. Any comparison to Jesus is underwhelming and retrofitted. Any reading of the Old Testament without the beer-goggles of Christianity leaves you expecting a warrior king who would lead the Jews to victory over the Romans, or Syrians, or Babylonians, or whoever was oppressing them at the time of the prophecy.

    Second, Bowtie was also predicted in the Old Testament. Perhaps you forget how Passover is all about unleavened bread? What is unleavened bread but a *wheat-based food that is un-risen*!

Endnotes:

[i] **Gospel of Newt:** *Thetans*

According to Scientology, a thetan is an immortal soul or spirit that uses the physical brain as a switchboard or control center to animate the human body. You, the reader, the mind imagining the words you are reading, are a thetan. The physical body holding this book is just an avatar it uses to interact in the physical world. An immortal thetan accumulates thoughts and memories throughout its billions of years of existence, even though we can't seem to remember them now. This means that modern psychology and psychiatry can't treat human mental problems because it only assumes your baggage comes from events in this life, or from damage to the physical brain.

The thetans on earth are left over from when Xenu, the leader of the Galactic Confederacy, brought billions of his people to earth 75 million years ago on spacecraft that looked like DC-8s just to stack them around volcanoes and blow them up with hydrogen bombs. It is unclear as to why he couldn't have just blown them up on a more nearby planet or moon, or why the volcanoes were necessary given that hydrogen bombs would do the trick all by itself, I would think.

I know, it sounds pretty crazy to me, too. Give me that old-fashioned Flying Spaghetti Monster religion anytime.

[ii] **Gospel of Greenbeard:** *Mind-Body Dualism*

Mind-body dualism is the basic idea of a soul which survives independent of the body, with most religions positing that it lives on in an afterlife following the death and decay of the physical body, and sometimes a pre-life prior to birth, and sometimes an endless or nearly endless cycle of reincarnation.

It used to be that people did not distinguish between a natural world and a supernatural world. It all just blended from one to the other. Heaven and Hell were physical places that you could go to if you had the wings or a shovel and knew where to dig. Greek gods lived at the top of the fairly inaccessible Mount Olympus. Lightning bolts were visible manifestations of supernatural origin.

It was only with science that we began to divide the supernatural from the natural. If it was measurable in some way, it was part of the natural world that we can describe by predictable (even if chaotic) formulas. Gravity, atoms, electromagnetic radiation, thermal dynamics, the nuclear reactions at the heart of the sun. One after another, these things became describable in natural terms. The remaining "supernatural" occurrences receded to unverifiable, unrepeatable anecdotes which can usually be explained by human nature and the natural deception our brains play on us.

Thus was born naturalism, the idea that the supernatural world was all in our imagination all along. The naturalist starts with the assumption that there is only the natural world. We assume that only that which we can measure or deduce from observation actually exists. This follows Occam's Razor, which advises us to go with the explanation which requires the least assumptions. It is a big assumption to posit a supernatural world existing alongside our own. When someone claims to have seen a ghost, we can either assume the person is lying (common enough), deceived by some natural phenomenon (happens all the time and is further clouded by emotional reaction), or that there exists a whole parallel universe which pokes through under spurious conditions but can never be verified scientifically.

Neuroscience shows us that all we are, our personality, our memories, our inclinations, all are affected by the physical structures in our brains. Even out-of-body experiences can be induced by drugs or electrical stimulation, with no credible accounts (upon investigation) of experiences that could not have happened any other way than for the spirit to leave the body. There is no need to assume, nor evidence for, a mind that exists beyond the physical brain.

[iii] **Gospel of Greenbeard:** *Free Will*

Theologically, the notion of free will claims that we are responsible for our own moral choices based on three aspects: external control, coercion, and a soul independent of the physical body.

It is free will if we make a choice with no external agent (God) compelling us beyond our control. "God did not make you do it." This is a problem. If God knew all your decisions ahead of time, we cannot deviate from the plan. We have no free will because all our choices are a predetermined fate, not only from our moment of birth, but from the beginning of time. This is a tenet of Calvinism. It is as though we are bowling balls where the bowler could throw a strike every time but purposely misses, knowing exactly which pins will fall beforehand. Much of Abrahamic religion tries to either ignore this problem or claims that somehow God blinded himself to your pre-destination.

It is free will if we make a choice with no external agent (God) coercing us. "God does not reveal himself to us because he wants us to have free will." This would imply that the most moral person is an atheist who behaves well, rather than one who behaves well out of fear of punishment (coercion). This conflicts with the Abrahamic god who wants you to believe in him and no other, and threatens to burn you in Hell for not doing so.

It is free will if our spiritual entity (soul) can make conscious choices independently of our physical bodies. Beyond the religious acknowledgement of the temptation of the flesh, this would imply that drugs and physical damage to the brain would not affect our choices, so I find this concept is demonstrably false.

Since nothing theological is testable, or even measurable, except where evidence seems to disprove the theological claim, there is no grounds for any serious discussion of these ideas. If it is measurable and testable, it moves into the realm of science and naturalism.

Naturalists, from an atheistic, non-supernatural worldview, often claim that there is no such thing as free will on the grounds of the third assumption (that the soul makes choices independent of the physical body). And this is sound reasoning if we stick with the theological definition. But if we consider free will as our choices made independently of external control and coercion, and employing a conscious, rational thought process in the physical structures of the brain, then it is certainly possible. It is all in how we define it.

It is free will when we make choices without outside control. In other words, there are no mind-control rays or drugs at work to influence our physical thought process. This is true most of the time for most people.

It is free will when we make choices free of coercion. We could consider societal norms, family dynamics, peer pressure, and penal codes all forms of coercion, so it may be the nature of the choice and the degree of coercion at work that determines just how free the will is in any given situation. But again, it is clear we make many decisions free of coercion.

It is in the third aspect, the meat-based thought process revealed by neuroscience, that we have any debate about what constitutes free will: *It is free will if we are not simply automatons (zombies) and we are capable of rationally thinking through our choices.* In this case, free will falls on a spectrum depending on the balance of *conscious will* to *urge*, and only applies where conscious reasoning has been applied. Neuroscience tells us that many of our actions are performed in zombie mode by unconscious subprocesses in our brains, and free will is not applicable in these cases. And our awareness itself is on the tail end of a long chain of neurologic events. But we make lots of choices where we rationally consider the information on hand and consult our own moral code and values, and choose accordingly, fully aware of at least the main influences of why we are making the choice we do. I would love a glass of scotch right now, but I won't, because I am trying to limit it to three nights a week for health and budget reasons.

Are we capable of some degree of conscious, rational thought? If we were not, then science would not work. Cognitive behavioral therapy (CBT) would not work. I would not work. For the most part, I don't plan my workday based on my emotions, which are telling me to go seize the day fishing. I plan it according to the requirements of my job, the maintenance of which is necessary to pay my mortgage. We are capable of rational thought because science works. CBT works. And I have not been fired yet. Therefore, I conclude that we have free will in this sense.

And this sense of free will is useful, as it can be used in consideration of culpability and moral assessment. The rational thought process, or executive function, is an emergent quality of evolutionarily advanced brains, a step beyond the zombie processes that provide most of our day-to-day animation. Even chimpanzees make sure no one is looking when they steal a banana. Not all criminals can control their impulses, but most attempt their deeds with the rational intent of cheating the system and not getting caught.

For most people, most of our moral choices involve at least some degree of free will, and some degree of involuntary influence outside of the conscious executive function. With the practiced discipline of critical thinking or the application of cognitive behavioral therapy, we can effectively push ourselves in the direction of free will.

Finally, some have promoted a hypothesis of free will based on quantum uncertainty. (The indeterministic nature of subatomic particles provides a gap for what?) It's a silly argument, usually put forward by people who don't understand quantum physics or neurology. As tiny as neurons are, they are still well above the quantum weirdness threshold. Even if quantum uncertainty affected our synapses, it would cause a morally irrelevant randomness rather than rational thought.

iv **Gospel of Greenbeard:** *Taurocoprology*
Taurocoprology: The science of bullshit.
- The first law: Falsifiability is a liability.
- The second law: One can't bullshit a bullshitter unless the bullshitter has bullshitted him- or herself.
- The third law: The effectiveness of scientific jargon is inversely proportionate to the scientific literacy of the target audience.

Famous taurocoprologists include James Randi, Joe Nickell, and Steven Novella, who use their knowledge to expose the bullshitters. Others such as Sylvia Browne, John Edward, and Uri Geller have gone to the dark side, which is far more lucrative. Donald Trump is a pseudo-taurocoprologist, being unskilled in his prodigious and transparent use of bullshit on the one hand and believing his own bullshit on the other.

v **The Unnatural Acts of the A-Pastas:** *Why are there still apes?*
Anyone with even a rudimentary understanding of Evolution should be able to answer this one, so only someone who has never learned anything about Evolution would be asking the question, and therefore is in no position to argue against it. But if you have a hard time explaining it, ask the person this: "If bulldogs were bred from other dogs, then why aren't all dogs now bulldogs?"

vi **Unnatural Acts/The Monk of San Marino:** *Non-biological Consciousness*
I leave this one to the philosophers to hash out. Is there a difference between a biological brain with self-awareness and a self-aware synthetic neural network? Does self-awareness constitute sentience? Can we ever know?

vii **The First Email of Tortellini to Vermicelli:** *Psychic Research*
Professor Daryl Bem of Cornell University conducted an experiment which garnered a lot of press coverage to test if subjects would react with heightened emotional response to disturbing images milliseconds before being exposed to them as they randomly flashed on a screen interspersed with emotionally neutral images. The problem is that the statistical measurement was just barely above random chance, and other researchers have not been able to reproduce the effect. We see a

repeating laboratory phenomenon: researchers who believe in psychic ability find positive results where other researchers don't. There are many ways to skew experimental results, and when skeptics or peer reviewers investigate, they often find subtle, unintentional manipulation of the data, as well as intentional deception.

Who wouldn't love to discover a major and revolutionary fact about our world like genuine psychic ability? Why would a negative-nelly skeptic attempt to suppress the truth? Some years ago, we saw a report claiming to measure neutrinos traveling faster than the speed of light. In all fairness, the scientists who reported it were asking for help in finding their flaw. I loved the idea of faster-than-light neutrinos, but I love the truth even more, and when it was determined that there was an unaccounted-for delay in the measurement due to a loose fiber optic cable, the boring old cosmic speed limit was preserved.

Extraordinary claims require extraordinary evidence, a thorough review of the experimental methodology, and replication by independent researchers.

[viii] **II Akronites:** *U.S. Government suppression of WHO report*
See https://www.theguardian.com/society/2003/apr/21/usnews.food
Also google the Sugar Research Foundation and read the NPR articles.

[ix] **II Akronites:** *Antioxidants*
A major follow-up study on antioxidants found that consuming fruits and vegetables with natural antioxidants (and fiber, and nutrients, and a low glycemic index) is healthy. However, consuming supplements too high in antioxidants may *increase* rates of cancer. The overabundance of environmental antioxidants from the supplements appears to cause cells to stop producing their own organic antioxidants which leads to an increase in free radicals. But the commercials continue. There is too much money to be made off the hype.

Check out https://nccih.nih.gov/health/antioxidants/introduction.htm for a summary of the science.

Bibliography

Alcock, James E. *Belief: What It Means to Believe and Why Our Convictions Are so Compelling.* Prometheus Books, 2018. eBook.

Darwin, Charles. *On the Origin of Species by Means of Natural Selection, or Preservation of Favoured Races in the Struggle for Life.* London: John Murray, 1859. Print.

Dawkins, Richard. *The Ancestor's Tale: A Pilgrimage to the Dawn of Evolution.* Boston: Mariner, 2005. Print.

Dawkins, Richard. *The Selfish Gene.* New York: Oxford University Press, 2007. Print.

Dennett, D. C. (Daniel Clement). *Consciousness Explained.* Boston: Little, Brown and Col, 1991. Print.

Denworth, Lydia. "I Feel Your Pain." *Scientific American* Dec. 2017: 58-63. Print.

Dreier, James. *Contemporary Debates in Moral Theory.* Blackwell, 2009. eBook.

Eagleman, David. *Incognito: The Secret Lives of the Brain.* Vintage Books, 2016. eBook.

Gell-Mann, Murray. *The Quark and the Jaguar: Adventures in the Simple and the Complex.* New York: W.H. Freeman, 1995. Print.

Harari, Yuval Noah. *Sapiens: a Brief History of Humankind.* Vintage, 2019. Audio.

Harms, Danilo, and Jason A. Dunlop. "A Revision Of The Fossil Pirate Spiders (Arachnida: Araneae: Mimetidae)." Palaeontology, vol. 52, no. 4, 12 Mar. 2009, pp. 779–802.

Harris, Sam. *Free Will.* Free Press, 2012

Hawking, Stephen. *A Brief History of Time.* New York: Bantam Books, 1996. Print.

Henderson, Bobby. *The Gospel of the Flying Spaghetti Monster.* New York: Villard Books, 2006. Print.

Lindsey P.A., Alexander R., Frank L.G., Mathieson A. & Romanach S.S. Potential of trophy hunting to create incentives for wildlife conservation in Africa where alternative wildlife-based land uses may not be viable. *Animal Conservation,* Aug. 2006: 283-291. Print.

Nahmias, Eddy. "Why We Have Free Will." *Scientific American* Jan. 2015: 77-80. Print.

Novella, Steven, and Bob Novella. *The Skeptics' Guide to the Universe: How to Know What's Really Real in a World Increasingly Full of Fake.* Grand Central Publishing, Hachette Book Group, 2018.

Our Continent: A Natural History of North America. Washington, D.C.: National Geographic Society, 1976. Print.

Prothero, Donald R. *Evolution: what the fossils say and why it matters.* New York: Columbia University Press, 2007. Print.

Reich David, Nick Patterson, Desmond Campbell, Arti Tandon, Stéphane Mazières, et al. Reconstructing Native American population history. *Nature*, Nature Publishing Group, 2012, 488 (7411), pp.370-4.

Sagan, Carl. *The Demon-Haunted World: Science as a Candle in the Dark.* New York: Ballantine Books, 1997. Print.

Sternberg, Eliezer J. *Neurologic: The Brain's Hidden Rationale behind Our Irrational Behavior.* New York: Pantheon Books, 2015. Print.

Translated by Joseph Smith, Jr. *The Book of Mormon.* Lamoni, Iowa: The Reorganized Church of Jesus Christ of Latter-Day Saints, 1874. Print.

Wilson, Edward O. *On Human Nature.* Harvard University Press, 2004. eBook.

Zukav, Gary. *The Dancing Wu Li Masters: An Overview of the New Physics.* New York: Perennial Classics, 2001. Print.

Acknowledgements

I wish to thank my wife for her patience during the long hours of work that went into this book, as well as her concern for my health, her wonderful sense of humor, and common sense feedback, all of which made me a better person if not a better writer. Thanks to Carl for providing the inspiration for the Littlest Pirate, as well as providing the Littlest Pirate herself. Thanks to Kris for the positive feedback and encouragement.

I also wish to thank the skeptic/atheist/humanist podcast community for being my constant companions over the past fifteen years in a world where the skeptical atheist humanist can feel pretty lonely at times. You guys rock.

Made in United States
North Haven, CT
25 March 2023

34541095R00104